# TRUST without BORDERS

A 40-Day Devotional Journey to
Deepen, Strengthen, and Stretch Your Faith in God

## Arabah Joy

D1056097

Copyright © 2014 by Arabah Joy. All rights reserved.
ISBN-13: 978-1499638806
ISBN-10: 1499638809

No part of this book may be reproduced, scanned, or distributed in any printed or electronic form without permission. The only exception is for short excerpts that include full reference to the book and author. If sharing a short excerpt online, the author's website (www.arabahjoy.com) must also be included in the reference. Please do not participate in or encourage piracy of copyrighted materials in violation of the author's rights.

Unless otherwise indicated, Scripture quotations are taken from the NEW AMERICAN STANDARD BIBLE®(NASB), Copyright © 1960,1962,1963,1968,1971,1972,1973,1975,1977,1995 by The Lockman Foundation. Used by permission.

Scripture quotations marked NIV are taken from THE HOLY BIBLE, NEW INTERNATIONAL VERSION®, NIV® Copyright © 1973, 1978, 1984, 2011 by Biblica, Inc.® Used by permission. All rights reserved worldwide.

Scripture quotations marked NET are from the NET Bible® copyright ©1996-2006 by Biblical Studies Press, L.L.C. http://netbible.com Scripture quoted by permission. All rights reserved.

Scripture quotations marked ESV are taken from The Holy Bible, English Standard Version® (ESV®), copyright © 2001 by Crossway, a publishing ministry of Good News Publishers. Used by permission. All rights reserved.

Scripture quotations marked AMP are taken from the Amplified® Bible, Copyright © 1954, 1958, 1962, 1964, 1965, 1987 by The Lockman Foundation Used by permission." (www.Lockman.org)

Scripture quotations marked HCSB are taken from the Holman Christian Standard Bible®, Copyright © 1999, 2000, 2002, all 2003 by Holman Bible Publishers. Used by permission. Holman Christian Standard Bible®, Holman CSB®, and HCSB® are federally registered trademarks of Holman Bible Publishers.

# Contents

# Introduction

They say we each have a signature sin. You know, like a chef's specialty dish, one of those things that differentiates you from the others. There is one particular sin that defines you and makes you. The one you turn to again and again, the one you've developed to ugly perfection.

My signature sin is unbelief. Yes, I've been soul-shaped by doubt. Distrust. Insecurity.

It's one of those sins common to women and men, and it goes all the way back to the beginning, straight back to Eve. That little seed of doubt planted in the heart of a woman was all the serpent needed to cause the whole of mankind to fall.

It's no wonder this particular temptation is a favorite weapon of our enemy. If our own personal history isn't proof enough, the effectiveness of doubt lines page after page of the Bible with a deadly dual strategy: to mock God and keep His children from entering the promised land.

Unbelief keeps us from loving others, sharing Christ, taking risks, giving ourselves away, and praying God's truth. It keeps us bound in our mediocrity. During His earthly ministry, Jesus made a few startling statements about how our faith affects the events of our lives, such as, "Let it be done to you according to your faith." Make no mistake about it: this signature sin of unbelief marginalizes our spiritual potential.

With this marginalizing, destructive sin so prevalent in my own life, I've long wondered how to replace it with faith. How does one stop committing their own signature sin?

Surely there are many answers to this question—some lengthy, some short. Yet the answer I needed to hear first came one day while my youngest son watched *Bob the Builder*, a film he had received for his birthday. Bob, the expert builder, retells the story of how he started and explains how he went from a completely incapable helper to an experienced pro.

There's one word for it—Practice.

We all learn the same way Bob did, by getting our hands dirty and practicing, day after day. Each day we show up and practice new things, and then do it again five minutes later. Repetition is the golden key.

We learn to flex our faith muscles through practice. Since faith without works is dead, then what if we, through practicing together, put feet on our faith and built into our lives the habit of trust? What if our faith quickened and rose to life with the habit of practice? When the anxiety pounds and we want to retreat, we practice stepping out, and forging ahead anyway. When life overwhelms and the way is dark, we refrain from lighting our own candles to practice relying on our God instead.[1] When the child seems lost and our own strength isn't enough, we trust God is faithful and He will do it.[2] When things look hope-

---

[1] Isaiah 50:10
[2] 1 Thessalonians 5:24

less in the land of famine, we practice picking up the oil jar and pouring that last bit out *anyway.*[3]

We *practice* faith and we *live* trust.

This compilation is not written from a position of strength, but of weakness. I write about trust because I know my signature sin and I do not want to be handicapped by it. I don't want it to define me. I write as an exercise of faith, as a way to combat distrust. I write to ponder how trust as a lifestyle works itself out, to show what it looks like in the kitchen, on the crowded city bus, and in the work place. I write to switch my life lens to one focused on our great God and who He describes Himself to be.

The Gospel of John is a book "written so that you might believe" (John 20:31). I find it motivating that God saw the struggles of the doubter—those who, like me, grapple hard to trust. God did not leave the doubter flailing in a state of distrust, but found a way to reach out and redeem them—us—from our sin, the sin of unbelief. He allowed such a gospel to come to us, so we might believe.

Each day of this devotional begins with a scripture reading from the book of John. My prayer for you is that you will be filled with faith in your inner being as you read words intended to impart trust.

---

[3] 2 Kings 4:1-7

## The 40 Day Just Trust Challenge

This book is more than a devotional. It is an invitation to make trust a habit. To this end, I have prepared 40 Daily Challenges to accompany the devotions found in this book. These bite-sized challenges are intended to give you hands on practice in trusting God. I encourage you to deepen, strengthen, and stretch your faith by making daily choices to put your trust in action. As a fellow sojourner, I wanted to make the daily challenges personal, with a real time and place for us to connect. Therefore, I am very happy to announce the challenges are available via podcast! You can access the Daily Challenges by subscribing to the Trust Without Borders Podcast on iTunes or visit my podcast page at:

www.arabahjoy.com/podcast/ for more information.


**"May the God of hope fill you with all joy and peace *as you trust in Him."* (Romans 15:13, NIV)**

# ~Day 1~

# Retreat

**"The light shines in the darkness,
and the darkness has not overcome it."
(John 1:5, ESV)**

"We're sending you guys to a bed and breakfast for two nights. We'll even take care of childcare." Pastor says this to my husband, Jackson, and me on a Tuesday as we stand there shocked and delighted. When Friday comes, we drop the kids off, pack our suitcase and drive an hour to the B&B.

It's while standing in the kitchen with our host, Steve, that we know. We aren't here simply for a getaway. God has sent us on a mission.

"My friend William is here," Steve tells us. "We won't get in your way. He stopped by here to say goodbye. You see, he's on his way out to the mountains of Colorado. He's got hot spots all over his body and doesn't have much longer. He's headed out there to die, alone." Steve explains as he shows us to our room.

William makes himself scarce. We try all day Saturday to connect with him but to no avail. Come Saturday night, we order Chinese takeout and sit on the bed, paper plates and chopsticks in hand, and talk about what we should do.

"I say let's go down and just tell them we don't believe in coincidence, and ask to pray for each of them. You know, see what the Lord does from there," I suggest.

My husband, his fire is burning. He wants to just go down with his Bible open and lay it all out. "Whatever the case, there will not be a natural opening. If we want to talk to William, we'll have to take the dreaded obvious and direct route."

We finish Chinese takeout with fortune cookies and my husband cracks his open. He reads, "Don't wait for others to open the right doors for you." We laugh.

"There you have it." I joke. "We have to go knock on William's door. The fortune cookie said so!"

We head downstairs, our Bibles tucked under our arms, only to find the two men gone, nowhere to be found. We finally find them outside in the cold, dark October night. We approach them to chat and ask if we can share breakfast with them in the morning because we'd like to pray with them and talk to them about God. Awkward and direct, we just lay it out. I'm sure we look like a couple of Bible thumpers with the social skills of rhinoceroses, but the two agree. It's clear they're just being polite and we wonder if they'll really show up at the breakfast table.

*Did we do the right thing?* I wonder.

But come 8:30 Sunday morning, the four of us sit down together for breakfast.

"This is only the third or fourth time I've ever sat down with guests," Steve tells us and we share some missionary stories and language blunders and we all laugh pretty good.

Then we get down to business. We ask William about his relationship with Jesus.

"You know," he begins. "I used to have faith. But some things happened in my life that made me wonder if what I had was real. People done me wrong. I've lost absolutely everything. The only thing I have left is a guitar and my old truck, and now I have to sell my guitar." He continued, "I read through the Bible in search of some foundation. I needed to know if what I thought I had was real. I came to the conclusion that I don't have real faith."

What he says next causes my eyes to well up and I don't really fight against it, because when the love of Christ comes out, people, well, they need to see it.

William reasoned, "I think I'm one of those that have to be slaughtered for someone else to be saved. You know, like in the book of Job, all his children were killed for Job to see and know God better. God's going to do what God wants to do and I'm one not intended for His blessing."

He stops for a bit, then continues. "I'm okay with it if that's the way it's supposed to be."

My heart is shattered and I can't believe what I'm hearing. "I'm not one of the elect," he concludes.

Steve chimes in. "I feel the same way. What if I'm an Esau? You know the part that says, 'Jacob have I loved, Esau have I hated'?"

We sit there sort of stunned. Jackson, my husband, turns to me because he knows me. He asks, "Do you want to share anything?"

Yes, I do want to say something. It's burning within me. It's so close to my heart, my breathing shallows and my pulse pounds and oh, I get this.

"There's a reason he asked if I want to say something," I begin, trying to catch my breath. "It's because he knows I've struggled with the same things."

I wonder how I can boil everything down to a simple conclusion. How can I talk about stumbling and distrust and wondering if God really loves you? About dark nights when you thought you had something with God and then an earthquake shatters and shakes you to the core? About wondering if you were ever founded on the right foundation in the first place? I take a deep breath. Everyone is looking at me, waiting. The weight of responsibility for the right words weighs heavy on my shoulders. How can I ever say the right thing?

"You know John the Baptist?" I ask them. "How he spent his entire life preaching Jesus and then he was arrested? I mean, here's a guy who from the womb was connected to Christ. His life's purpose was to proclaim the Lamb of God. Then he finds himself in prison and, while there in the darkness, waiting for his head to be served on a platter, he begins to wonder, what if everything he had believed his entire life was a lie? In that dark hour, he sent one last, faltering message to Jesus. Shaken to his core, broken, he asked just one thing. **'Are you really the One?'**"[4]

I watch their faces intently before continuing.

"John was a man whose faith was rocked to the core. His very life hung in the balance; everything he thought he knew and believed was shifting. He was in a very stormy place. What Jesus said is very interesting. He told John to evaluate things on the basis of scripture, not his personal circumstances.

"But then He said something very important. Something so brief, it's easy to miss. **He said, 'Blessed is the one who does not stumble on account of Me.'**[5] I looked up that word 'stumble' and did a word study. I was at a place of doubt, stormy and afflicted, a stumbling place in my own faith. And this is what I found that changed everything for me…"

*{We will continue our conversation with Steve and William tomorrow. Can you relate to John the Baptist? What about William and Steve? Have circumstances or other people caused you to stumble in your faith? If so, there's good news for you! Stumbling doesn't have to be permanent! We will pick up with this amazing truth tomorrow.}*

---

[4] Matthew 11:3
[5] Matthew 11:6

*TRUST without BORDERS*

# ~Day 2~

# Scandalous

**"No one has seen God at any time; the only begotten God who is in the bosom of the Father, He has explained Him."**
**(John 1:18)**

Steve and William are looking at me, listening intently, wondering exactly what earth-shattering truth I had discovered. I'd entered that dark, cold prison cell with John the Baptist. With him, I'd asked, "Are You really the One?" I'd agonized. I'd wondered if I was really His. *I'd doubted God.* I'd done the opposite of what Jesus said the blessed ones do.[6]

"My faith was obliterated," I tell them. "I needed to know where that left me. Was I shipwrecked? So I did a word study on that word 'stumble.' I found it is not a general word for sin, but instead refers to a very specific condition. **It means 'to cease believing.'**

"In fact, one Bible dictionary says the word means, 'to cause a person to distrust One who is worthy of complete trust and obedience.'

"It's what Jesus said *not* to cause in children.[7]

"Furthermore," I continue, "it is the word Jesus used when He went to the cross. He said all of the disciples would 'fall away.' Same word. See, Jesus said even the disciples would stumble in their faith. And Jesus told Peter, 'Satan

---

[6] Matthew 11:2-6
[7] Mark 9:42

has asked to sift you like wheat. But I have prayed for you, *that your faith would remain (not stumble)*. And when you have returned, strengthen your brethren."[8]

I look into their faces, my own eyes wet, hoping they feel the release of just this: "Stumbling doesn't have to be permanent," I whisper. "When it all comes down, regardless of what evil has been done to us, no matter what dark nights we have seen, no matter the fear and loneliness, no matter our own faithlessness and falling away, the depth of our sinfulness – it all comes down to *His* character. In the end, it isn't about us at all. It's about Him, and His name is Faithful."

I don't know how they understand the weak attempt I make, but they do. Jackson takes over and explains the love of God for another hour or more. He shares how God was demonstrating His love that very moment, in bringing all of us to this same place at this same time, out of every place we could and should be, the globe over; yet He orchestrated each of our lives so we could be together, in order for us to know His hope and grace and speak together of His love.

"He loves you. He wants you to believe it," Jackson pleads as one given the ministry of reconciliation. He quotes John 3:16, a simple statement, yet so rich.

Later that day, after we've hugged William's neck and prayed for them both, and after we've slipped a twenty dollar bill in the dashboard of William's old truck as a small expression of God's love, we leave the B&B and return home to our own babes, noise, and busyness.

"What did the Lord say to you through all that?" Jackson asks me.

"I'm not sure yet," I tell him. "I need to think about it."

---

[8] Luke 22:31-32

I think about what had happened to William. I think about what happened to me as a child. I think about my adopted Little Bit and the hard place she has come from, the trauma that still marks her. I think about the headlines of the day, the depths of pain, sin, and heartache.

And I think about what persecution did to John the Baptist, what disillusionment did to the disciples, and what oppression did to the Israelites. In each case, it skewed their perspective of *God.* It caused them to stop believing. I think about the myriad of things that cause us to withdraw, reject, and stop believing in God's perfect, unconditional love for us.

And then it hits me. That word for "stumble"? The word that means to cease trusting the One who is absolutely worthy and deserving of our complete trust and obedience? It's the word "skandalizo" in Greek.

As in *scandal.*

And the Spirit that enlightens hearts shines deep in my soul and brings understanding. I know how to answer Jackson's question. I know what it is God wants to say to me.

**"It's not what is done to you that is scandalous, My child. It is never what happens in life that is scandalous. *Distrust for Me is the real scandal.*"**

Distrust for God is what causes heavenly hosts to cover their eyes, to brings hands to mouth aghast. This is what causes those who stand in God's presence and who know God's good and holy nature to draw back in horror: *when one of us on earth distrusts Him.*

I review my life. I think of the abuse I experienced as a child. As wrong and terrible as that was, the real scandal was when I responded in distrust against God. I think about hardship, pain, trauma, rejection, abuse, neglect, poverty, and deep suffering the world over. And yet still the real scandal in the truest sense is when our response is distrust for the Holy One who is absolutely and eternally trustworthy.

Distrust really is the real scandal. Because the sufferings of this world don't compare to the glory of Him. Oh, if we could just see!

**"Blessed indeed is he who does not stumble on account of Me."**[9]

Isn't this why Satan attacks our faith and starts even with the youngest of children? He wants to blind our eyes with pain. He wants to mar our vision with abuse, neglect, and hardship. He wants to keep our eyes on our failures and sin, on everything that's wrong instead of on the One and Only who is right.

He wants to scandalize the One who should never, ever, ever be doubted, the One who demonstrated the depths of His character by entering the womb of a woman, being cared for by the hands of sinful man, making Himself vulnerable in a world of sin, and finally dying at the hands of us all. Oh yes, Satan wants to establish early on a lifestyle of truly scandalous living through distrust of One whose very name is Faithful and True.

There in the kitchen, I drop to my knees and pray to the Holy One who is worthy. *"Oh my God, may I never scandalize You again!"* And I pray for a man named William, a man traveling deep into a Colorado winter towards a painful, lonely death. "May he be saved," I pray. "May You find him. May his dark, cold prison of death be where he discovers Your faithfulness, Your trustworthiness. And may his stumbling turn to faith."

---

[9] Matthew 11:6

I sense His whispered response reverberating deep within me. "Strengthen the brethren, my child. Strengthen the brethren."[10]

---

[10] Luke 22:32

# ~Day 3~

# Awakened

**"And this is eternal life, that they know you the only true God, and Jesus Christ whom you have sent."**
**(John 17:3, ESV)**

I still remember the moment it happened, the single comment that changed everything, the moment of truth that jarred me awake. It had been a long day. The kids were down for the night, my husband was out, and I was in the kitchen alone on the other side of the world, standing barefoot and pregnant at the sink, the back door propped open with a jug of laundry detergent, begging a breeze in.

It was stifling hot.

And there I was, scrubbing caked food off of high chair trays. I popped earbuds in, trying to learn all I could from those who had gone before, trying to imitate those who through faith and patience inherited promises. In reality, I was just trying to figure out how to do this thing called the Christian life.

I had downloaded content from the internet, blessed gift, my cord of connection to the outside world. Derwin Gray was sharing his testimony, but it was God who had a message for me. The words that came from Derwin's mouth pierced such that they lodged in my memory. Any momma realizes how significant that is for the mommy brain who'd just put the cheese in her purse instead of in the fridge. And Derwin Gray, on that stifling hot night a world away, said, "A false god is never satisfied."

Six simple words had never rocked my world before like these words did. Piercing, shaking me up, turning me inside-out to expose what I already suspected: the god I worshiped, the one I thought was God Almighty, may not be the One True God. Just like the disciples walked with Jesus but didn't know Him. Just how God's people in Isaiah didn't know their Redeemer. Maybe, just maybe, I didn't really know God either.

Can we be Christ followers but not God knowers?

"Jesus said to him, 'Have I been with you so long, and you still do not know me, Philip?'" (John 14:9, ESV)

Like Philip, I knew what every other Christ follower knows about God. I could quote verse after verse and understood Jesus to be the Messiah, the Son of God. But in the gut, the soul, despite all my knowledge, I didn't understand the *heart* of God. I didn't trust His intentions. When the winds blew (and they did) and the earth shook (and it did), I wasn't so sure God would come through for me.

I thought I understood Him. Yet an honest look at my behavior reflected an impotent, weak God, one who was never satisfied. I began to wonder if maybe I was like Philip, a Christ follower who didn't really understand the nature of God.

Scripture says God *is* satisfied. On the cross, Christ said, "It is finished." He fulfilled Heaven's demands Himself. He took our sin problem into His own hands so that once and for all it would be completed. The job would be accomplished without risk of failure and afterwards, King Jesus sat down at the right hand of the Father as an act of cessation.

He still sits. It's still finished. The end.

That night standing barefoot at a sink of tepid dishwater in an overseas kitchen, I understood one thing. The god I worshiped as God, the one that never seemed satisfied, was actually only a god made in the image of man, shaped and defined by my life experiences. My view of God had been shaped by savvy personalities entering and exiting my life, by authority figures I unquestioningly accepted, by my own emotional experiences. Like each of us, I've been a beneficiary of views, ideas, assumptions, and notions about God passed down from a myriad of sources, a toxic concoction of worthless with a dash of truth mixed in.

Is it any wonder we don't trust?

You can't trust a God you don't *really* know, in actuality. **And you can't leave knowing God to happenstance.**

That's what I learned that night in the kitchen. Jonah 1:4 describes it well. "The Lord hurled a violent wind on the sea, and such a violent storm arose on the sea that the ship threatened to break apart. The sailors were afraid, and each cried out to his god" (HCSB).

God sends the storm to reveal our false notions about Him. No, it doesn't look gracious, but it is. He doesn't send the storm to shipwreck us. He sends it to show that the god we call on is not God at all. In the storm, we finally call out to the one true God, to Yahweh. And He answers.

When He does, we know God like never before and we fear the Lord even more, offering sacrifices and vows.[11]

The storm of stumbling is not meant to shipwreck us but to give us sight. It opens the door to intimacy with a God we only thought we knew. The storm strips us of falsehood and invites us to one thing: to no longer leave knowing God to happenstance.

---

**"So realize that the LORD your God is the true God, the faithful God who keeps  covenant faithfully with those who love him and keep his commandments, to a thousand generations."**

**(Deuteronomy 7:9, NET)**

---

[11] This was the response of those on the terrifying boat ride in Jonah 1.

# ~Day 4~

# Trash Diggers

***"... and you will know the truth,
and the truth will make you free."***
**(John 8:32)**

I watch the old lady pick through trash cans, methodically separating the cardboard and plastic from the rest of the smelly garbage. It's a way for her to make a few extra dollars each week, a way to put a bowl of steaming rice porridge on her table. So every morning, she digs what's valuable from the rubbish.

My life is different from hers. Cardboard is worthless to me. I have no use for broken glass. But if my faith is going to be restored, it's time I sort through some rubbish myself, garbage of a different sort. Jeremiah 15:19 speaks, instructing me, "If you extract the precious from the worthless, you will be My spokesman."

This verse was written to Jeremiah, the prophet of God. If anyone should have his spiritual act together, you would think it'd be someone like Jeremiah. Yet God's word to Jeremiah was that in order to be God's spokesman, he needed to address an issue in his life. He needed to extract from the rubbish and debris that which precious.

We all possess a mixture of valuable and worthless beliefs. This is especially important to understand when it comes to our beliefs about God. We are all beneficiaries, both of worthy, and worthless, ideas about God. It was A.W. Tozer, in fact, that said the greatest thing about a person is how she thinks about God.

Just as our physical eyes perceive and interpret our surroundings, our spiritual eyes perceive and interpret life, ourselves, and God. Our spiritual perspective is how we understand and relate with God.

**It can be accurate or it can be dead wrong.**

Jesus tells us the condition of our spiritual eye is vitally important and urges us to make sure it is healthy.

**"Your eye is the lamp of your body. When your eyes are healthy, your whole body is full of light. But when they are unhealthy, your whole body also is full of darkness. See to it, then, that the light within you is not darkness." (Luke 11:34-35, NIV)**

It is possible that our spiritual eye can be underdeveloped. It can be immature. It can be damaged or diseased. **Yet the shocking reality is that most of us have never challenged our spiritual perceptions.** We've never questioned our assumptions about God, ourselves, or how we perceive life itself.

Matthew 16:13-18 (NIV) records a conversation Jesus had with His disciples.

> *When Jesus came to the region of Caesarea Philippi, he asked his disciples, "Who do people say the Son of Man is?"*

> *They replied, "Some say John the Baptist; others say Elijah; and still others, Jeremiah or one of the prophets."*
>
> *"But what about you?" he asked. "Who do you say I am?"*
>
> *Simon Peter answered, "You are the Messiah, the Son of the living God."*
>
> *Jesus replied, "Blessed are you, Simon son of Jonah, for this was not revealed to you by flesh and blood, but by my Father in heaven.*

Jesus' questions get at the root of our belief system. Are our beliefs rooted in cultural Christianity? Are they inherited from our parents, or our church? Are they a conglomerate of teachings we've heard on the internet and over the radio? Are they simply our own opinions about God? Or have our beliefs about God been revealed to us by God Himself through His Word?

Hebrews 11:6 says this is the essence of faith: coming to God believing He is who and what He says He is, and trusting that He is a rewarder of those who seek Him.[12]

Trust begins here. We simply come to God and trust He is going to reward us because we are seeking Him. We trust *He really is that good.* Trust also calls us to sort through some rubbish. If people in our lives have taught us God is a stingy, rigid God, we toss that belief out because His Word says He is generous and demonstrates it every

---

[12] Many scholars believe this verse refers to God as "I AM," meaning we are not just to believe God exists, but believe that He is who He says He is. Refer to the American Standard Version of this verse.

day.[13] In His kindness and generosity, He faithfully causes the sun to shine on the good *and* the evil.

If our background says God is a weak God and we have to work really hard to keep our salvation, we reject that as a worthless belief because His Word says He is able to keep us from falling and to present us faultless in His presence.[14]

Perhaps you aren't sure where to begin in your journey to a deeper trust in God. If so, I encourage you to start here: simply trust that God is a rewarder of those who seek Him. Then go to Him in prayer and express your trust and your desire to know Him as He is. He will not fail you.

---

[13] Matthew 5:45
[14] Jude 24

# ~Day 5~

## The Shepherd

**"Of His fullness we have all received, and grace upon grace. For the law was given through Moses; grace and truth were realized through Jesus Christ."**
**(John 1:16-17)**

It's 3:22 a.m. Darkness seeps down hallways and into bedrooms and enters a little boy's sleep. I hear him cry out and Jackson is the first to jerk the blankets back and rush to his firstborn. I wonder at that, after things are quiet again, at how the terrifying things come at us in the dark, in our vulnerable moments. Always in the vulnerable.

And we feel weak, exposed, powerless. In our fear, we grapple for control. In our stumbling, we reach for strength. Mao Zedong said that power lies in the barrel of a gun. Dictators and kings, the strong, they've secured their strength on the backs of the weak. Guns are power; gold is power; knowledge is power; dynamite is power; ability or influence over others is power. We are a world of people grappling for control through whatever means we can find. We struggle to be strong.

But isn't it only the power*less* who use force?

Yes, I know it. In my own home, when the bickering starts and the needs and the demands and life are all coming hard and fast, I fall back on that which makes me feel strong: task-mastering. When I feel power*less*, I use force. I'm sick with it and my stomach revolts with the power-control cycle.

Truth is, some of us live this because we have believed this is power. We live it in our parenting and in our relationships and our own obedience to God, cracking the whip to maintain control. We believe it because we haven't known any different. Many of us believe this even about God. We've been hoodwinked into thinking God exerts His power through the driving slash of expectation, the harsh demands, the condemnation, the task-mastering, the high standards that keep pushing the broken forward. For some of us, it is all we've ever known about God.

The law.

Yes, the law is good and holy, but the law is, after all, only a tutor. And we've long been tutored under taskmasters. It's time for graduation, for the job of the tutor is simply to point us to something better, to graduate us into Christ.[15]

It's in Exodus that I see it, how God's people were driven and oppressed and afflicted hard. The fear of powerlessness had caused Egypt to find a way to stay strong: through the crack and slash of the whip. For 400 years, the Israelites had known Egypt's power, their bloody control through force.

So God stepped in. He reset the standard and showed us clear what the power of Creator King looks like. How? Get this, because it is important: **by sending a shepherd.**

To these people driven and forced, wounded and bruised, condemned and worn out, *God sent a shepherd*, carrying a single tool in his hands. It wasn't a whip or a gun or a

---

[15] Galatians 3:24

bag of gold, yet this tool would singlehandedly bring free-dom to an entire nation. *"Take up this staff, for with it you shall...do My wonders."*[16]

**A simple shepherd with a simple staff. That's God's way. When He wants to demonstrate His power most, He always sends a Shepherd.**

John 10 tells us about our Good Shepherd, One who doesn't drive, but leads. He doesn't force from behind, slashing a whip; He beckons from His position in front. "Come," He speaks. He leads us, not through control, but with His beloved voice.[17]

Real power is in the staff, never the whip.

*We can trust that kind of Power.*

I wonder if we've been lied to about God. Yes, He is thrice holy; He has a standard of perfection, which makes us deserving of condemnation that culminates in hell. But here's what Jesus came to reveal: the whip has nothing on the staff. The whip draws blood. But the staff? **It parts the waters.**

Mr. Mao, power does not lie in the barrel of the gun. Our God, who is power, came as the Good Shepherd, to lead us, guide us, and lay down His life for us.

That's the power of Love. And that kind of power is trust-worthy.

---

[16] Exodus 4:17
[17] John 10:27

"I am the Good Shepherd; the Good Shepherd lays down his life for the sheep."

(John 10:11)

# ~Day 6~

# The Supply Line

### "... the man believed the word
### that Jesus spoke to him."
### (John 4:50, ESV)

The kids and I drive downtown into the setting sun to hear about the Nuba people. We sing in Arabic and our Sudanese brothers teach us, "Yesu gouwa aswa gouwa." At least, that's how I sing it. Jesus is super, super power.

Three men report to our association of churches. They show videos of lorries filled with grain traveling through the rain into the Nuba mountains. We watch as the Nuba people come running. "Who sent this?" they ask. "Where does this come from and why?"

Our brothers, those three men sent out from our churches girded with the prayers of the brethren and enabled with support, they tell our oppressed brothers, "Your brothers and sisters in America have heard about you. They see your suffering and they love you and want you to know they care. They sent us to you with food and the love of Christ."

We witness tears, trickling down their faces as they receive food and hope. My cheeks are wet, too, as I watch the exchange, and we all bow low, basked in this glory. We watch sacks of grain go off the trucks, carried on shoulders into caves and crevices where mothers and children hide. Then the refugees pile in; over 500 people pack into those trucks, until they are forced to turn people away. Back down the mountain, through muck and checkpoints and darkness and danger, the trucks drive down to the nearest refugee camp.

We praise our Father for the success of the mission, and at the end of report time, the floor opens for questions. A woman stands up and asks if there is a way to send supplies, things like shoes and clothing. "I have a garage full of clothing I can't use," she says.

Pastor Tim says something that strikes the heart and lingers long. "It's not a matter of food and clothing being available. They have these things available and at far lower prices than we could ever get it to them at. Additionally, there are relief organizations on the ground and government agencies as well. **So it's not a matter of availability. It's that the supply lines are broken. They can't get the supplies up to them.**"

Pastor Tim explains how the enemy has come in and bombed the area, creating fear. The people are running for their lives, dispersed and scattered. The supply line necessary for transporting the resources has crumbled.

"There are people up there starving because there is no way to get the abundance of food in the city up the mountains into the caves," Pastor Tim concludes.

Long after the service is over, the Spirit speaks the words over and again to my heart. *"It's not a matter of availability. My grace is sufficient. But the supply line is down."*

**The supply line is down.**

The scriptures tell us how the enemy of our souls roams and roars like a lion.[18] He aims to ignite fear and we scatter and stumble. Our supply line is cut off. But aren't all the resources of Christ surely always available to us, just not always appropriated? Looking out over the mass of American believers, could it be said of many of us, that our supply line is down?

Yet there's this blinking headlight in the battle dark, the reminder that faith is the victory. For those cut off and holed up and without supply, this hope in the dark points the way. Faith is *the* victory that overcomes the world.[19] The believer's supply line is our faith.

Dr. Joon Gon Kim, founder of Campus Crusade's Korean ministry, is quoted in Vonette Bright's book, *In His Hands*, saying, *"Faith is the source of all graces that we receive. We are saved by faith. We live by faith. We pray by faith. We walk by faith. We appropriate the filling of the Holy Spirit by faith. By faith we overcome the world. All these blessings and virtues of the Christian life are rooted in faith."*[20]

I read it right there in Jude, the instruction to re-establish our supply lines. **If we are not fully appropriating the sufficiency of Christ, we must tend to our most holy faith.**

"But you, beloved, build yourselves up on your most holy faith [make progress, rise like an edifice higher and higher], praying in the Holy Spirit." (Jude 1:20, AMP)

---

[18] I Peter 5:8
[19] 1 John 5:4
[20] Bright, Vonette. *In His Hands,* Ventura, California: Regal, 2010

Later, the Nuba team tells us the plan to establish a church there at the base of those mountains. I can envision it. I see faith rising like an edifice, supply lines stretching from south to north, closing the gaps, connection re-established.

And with my own battle weary eyes I see it, a faith amongst God's children the globe over that appropriates all the sufficiency of Christ.

Yes, beloved ones, re-establish the supply line. Build yourselves up in your most holy faith.

---

# How to Build Faith

**"So faith comes from hearing, and hearing through the word of Christ." (Romans 10:17, ESV)**

A steady diet of God's Word is the foundation of faith. Do you have a Bible reading plan? For a list of resources I personally use and recommend, please visit my blog at www.arabahjoy.com/trust-resources. If you do not have a Bible reading plan, I encourage you to start yours today.

---

# ~Day 7~

## God's Intentions

**"For God did not send the Son into the world
to judge the world, but that the world
might be saved through Him."
(John 3:17)**

It's 4:54 a.m. and His voice comes softly, awakening me. *"Understand what the will of the Lord is."* I lay under the warm mountain of blankets for a while, pondering these words. I think of how my traditional upbringing taught me to understand the will of God in vague terms like glorifying God and obeying His commandments, as if I could if only I worked hard enough.

Surely obedience and glory are a part of His will, but broad strokes hold little meaning without the vibrant details of grace.

This particular morning, His words invite me to find articulation for something deeper, something more genuine, more guttural. Expression comes simply: **His will is not primarily the things I do.**

For the next three days, I pour over scriptures, receiving Jackson's help with the Bible study software. Slowly, deeper articulation forms. "Will" is "thelema" in Greek. It means desire, pleasure, intent. It is what one wishes or has determined shall be done. According to Ephesians 1, God's will is Christ slain before the foundation of the world. We could say in short, it is the purpose of God to bless mankind through Christ.

Think about it. God's will is to bless mankind through Christ. How skewed we are when we think of God's will simply in terms of what He desires *from* us. We must train ourselves to think first in terms of His *intentions towards* us. In this, Ephesians 1 is a gold mine. His will is "kind intentions" and "lavish grace."

It is here I discover that His will was to bless me with every spiritual blessing,

to choose me,

to consider me holy and blameless,

to adopt me,

to redeem me,

to forgive me all my transgressions,

to make me the recipient of His abounding grace,

to give me all wisdom and insight into His heart for me,

to give me an inheritance,

to grant me the fullness of His Spirit,

to rescue me from the domain of darkness and transfer me to the kingdom of His beloved Son,

to reconcile me to Himself,

to make me at peace with Him.

God's will, the deepest intentions of His heart, are not secret. He's not hiding some trick up His sleeve. We are not left to wonder if sinister motives drive His actions. He lays them all out in Ephesians 1.

After three days of cross referencing, pondering, and asking, it comes down to a little phrase buried in Colossians 4:12, *"Stand perfect and fully assured in all the will of God."*

When it comes down to understanding God's will for my life, from the messy momma mornings to the ministry pressures and the heartaches that take the breath away, I can stand perfect and full of assurance. **His intentions towards me are trustworthy.** This can be the rock underfoot, the breath, the blood, the life of the broken and struggling.

I can trust God's intentions.

I practice it. As kids wake up and need me, as I dress a tired and whiny little one, I practice standing perfect on these words: "I am fully assured in all the will of God. In all the messy and mundane of today, God is for me. I can do this. I can love and bless and give and pour out, because I am fully assured in all the will of God for me."

The spark of faith becomes a flame.

As an older child grumbles about changing a simple shirt: "I can do this. I can take aside and breathe life words into him, exhort him to live up to his identity in Christ as a beloved child. I can refuse frustration because God's will is that I be here, pouring life and truth and confidence into this child. I stand fully assured."

As time presses, stress rises, lunches need packing, dress pants need ironing, and children scatter toys, I simply, amazingly, say, "I can do this. I can focus on what really matters, standing in perfect confidence and assurance about all God's will for me."

These are mind-renewing, life-altering truths. No matter what comes my way today, I can trust. My assurance is not my ability or my savvy skills at maneuvering life. My assurance is that God's intentions towards me are pure, good, and right. Today, we can stand perfect and fully assured.

# ~Day 8~

# Redeemed from Empty

***"Jesus answered and said to her, 'If you knew the gift of God, and who it is who says to you, "Give me a drink," you would have asked Him and He would have given you living water.'"***
**(John 4:10)**

Five kids, one dirty dog, one messy house, and one demanding husband into life, she lost it.

I remember sitting in the van as a child while we drove her and her daughter to the ER. After seeing the doctor, she up and walked out of that ER loony.

She went missing and even after they found her and her frightened daughter on a dark street in downtown Tampa, it took a while for us to really *find* her. It was just like her mom before her, my grandmother, and her mom before her. Just like generations of moms past as far back as I can trace. I come from a long line of women who've lived their frailty, not always their faith, who've proven we're nothing but dust.

And for all this talk about trust, it can be terrifying to realize that we, **after all our tea parties and ironed dresses and Sunday smiles and churchy quips, are still children of Eve**. We are our mother's daughters, whose ancestral blood pulses through us with all its genetic disorder. We are daughters of alcoholic mothers. Abusive mothers. Unstable mothers. Unavailable mothers.

And sometimes, despite our best attempts at being good moms, when we get quiet we hear the thump of fallen human blood pumping through the veins, reminding us of who we are, threatening to destroy us.

We need the hope of redemption.

*"[For you know] that you were redeemed from the empty way of life handed down to you from your ancestors."* **(1 Peter 1:18-19)**

Truth is, we **have** the hope of redemption.

We can live the hope of redemption because redemption has been purchased for us. We trust because the One who promised is trustworthy. Hebrews 10:23 says, "Let us hold unwaveringly to the hope that we confess, for the One who made the promise is trustworthy" (NET).

When we wake up and walk weak, we need to be men and women who remember the gospel, a rag-tag band who preaches it to ourselves. Someone today needs to grab hold of it and never let go, because **there is one Name given under Heaven by which we can be saved, and He can be trusted**. His blood supersedes the blood we inherited from Eve.

The antidote to being a daughter of Eve is the *all-sufficient, perfect blood of Christ.* Apply it liberally when you itch to reach for that substance, when you're tempted to engage in self-gratification instead of being present for your kids, when you feel the anger rising, when you drive yourself with condemnation or more performance. Today, replace Eve's blood with Jesus' blood. Believe the gospel.

Let this pump through the veins: "I've been redeemed. I can live differently because I've been rescued from the worthless ways of my ancestors. The blood I've been redeemed with is perfect, without blemish or defect. It is sufficient!"

And today, live as one redeemed.

## For those who have never trusted Christ for redemption:

I am aware that perhaps someone reading this today longs for the redemption found in Christ but you have not trusted in Him for salvation. Scripture tells us there is no other name by which we can be saved apart from the name of Christ. This is because Jesus Christ was fully God and as such, was qualified to take our sin upon Himself.

Today, I'd like to share how you can become a Christian by trusting in Jesus Christ. The gospel is simply the good news that God made a way for us to be redeemed and made right with Him. Salvation involves several things. First, it involves an acknowledgement of your sin. In order to be redeemed, each of us must turn away from our own righteousness and confess our sin to God. Secondly, it involves turning towards Christ in faith. When we turn to Christ, it means we believe He alone is capable and sufficient to cleanse us of sin and make us right before God. Additionally, we believe He was willing to do so and demonstrated His loving intentions by coming to earth and taking our place in life and death. This trust occurs in our heart. And finally, salvation involves our mouths, making confession to God and others that we are relying on Christ and are submitting to His Lordship over our lives.

If you have never turned away from self and turned to Christ, I invite you to stop right now and ask Him to redeem you. Read through these Scriptures and allow Him to speak to you and show you the good news of the gospel!

Romans 3:10-12, 23

Romans 6:23

Romans 5:8

Romans 10:9-10

Romans 5:1

Romans 8:1

Romans 8:38-39

If you would like more information on becoming a Christian or have just trusted Christ, please visit me at my blog and drop me a note via the contact form. I'd love to hear from you! www.arabahjoy.com

# ~Day 9~

# Consider

**"Truly, truly, I say to you, he who hears My word
and believes Him who sent Me has eternal life,
and does not come into judgment but has
passed out of death into life."
(John 5:24)**

I imagine that maybe, just maybe, she was a woman like me. Because when she first heard the news, she laughed.[21] "Can't happen for me," she said.

In that, we are alike.

I'm not proud of the cynicism, the hard edge, the bracing against hope. And yet, if it could be part of her redemptive story, it's okay for it to be part of ours. There *is* hope. The hall of faith tells us that she believed God, but we know that for some time she didn't. First the laughter, the unbelief. Then the scheming, the taking matters into her own hands. Finally, the abuse.[22]

We mustn't forget that for a long time her story didn't read like she trusted.

Between the giving of a promise and the blossoming of faith there lies a dark territory, the howls of the soul, the dry barren ground that we each have to face in ourselves. The wretchedness of self that we'd prefer to hide, cover

---

[21] Genesis 18:11-12
[22] Genesis 16:1-2

up, deny, busy away with meaningless activity. Sarah's faith story teaches us trust is birthed when we finally see "the deadness of our womb,"[23] the sheer *impossibility* of ourselves.

This is where real faith is birthed, when we finally understand there is nothing in us to work with. Self esteem experts tell us to believe in ourselves, but faith says believe in God. Self talk gurus tout the importance of telling ourselves we are enough, but in actuality, we must be broken of self-effort, self-reliance, and self-righteousness before faith can be birthed. When the seed of self dies, new life springs forth, the beginnings of Divine promise.

Our spiritual mother walked these dark shadow lands of the soul and she made it out to stand beneficiary of all His promises. We can, too. Be assured the path will always expose our deadness and exposure makes just one demand: to contemplate the impossibility of self and lay it down. Just lay it down. Take up the way offered in its stead, the way of faith.

How did Sarah do it? How did she lay down her self-reliance, her rush to birth Ishmael, and take up trust instead? Perhaps she walked the path with Abraham, her husband. We have a record of his journey. This can become ours. It can become legacy.

---

[23] Romans 4:19-20

# Following Abraham's Process to Faith (Hebrews 11:19) A 10-Minute Practical Exercise in Trust

## Abraham *"considered"*

"Consider" is an action verb and means "to count, to calculate, to press your mind down upon." It's an accounting term that means to crunch and come to a solution. This is the activity of faith, this considering. This is a vital engagement of the mind, to sit down and calculate.

Go ahead and do it now: on a sheet of paper, list all the deadness of yourself, your inabilities, your limitations, your inadequacies that face you today. Then move on to the next section.

## He considered *that "God is able"*

Biblical "considering" focuses on the nature of God. Our faith is only as good as its object. Is your God too small? Is He impotent or powerful? Is He stingy or generous? Is He angry or quick to forgive? Is your understanding of God accurate? Time spent considering the attributes of God is time well spent.

A. W. Pink said:

> The incomprehensibility of the Divine nature is not a reason why we should desist from reverent inquiry and prayerful strivings to apprehend what

*He has so graciously revealed of Himself in His Word. Because we are unable to acquire perfect knowledge, it would be folly to say we will therefore make no efforts to attain to any degree of it. It has been well said (by Spurgeon) that,* **"Nothing will so enlarge the intellect, nothing so magnify the whole soul of man, as a devout, earnest, continued investigation of the great subject of the Deity."[24]**

On your paper, consider the ability and willingness of our God.

## He considered that God is able *"even to raise the dead"*

This little phrase is important because it shows that Abraham actively applied the character of God to his specific and individual circumstances. It does us the most good when we, too, take the nature of God and apply it to our situation.

Let me provide a personal example. When I wake up in the morning and feel the stress, here's how I can follow the steps of Abraham and choose faith:

> Lord, I know that You are with me wherever I go. I also know that You are helping me. (And here I might recite Isaiah 40:10-13.) I come to You to quench my thirst and satisfy my hunger. I trust You to direct my paths. You are my righteousness be-

---

[24] Pink, A.W. *The Attributes of God*, Kindle Edition: Chapel Library, 2012.

cause I am all out of my own goodness. You always lead me in triumph and my adequacy for this day comes from You. As I step out into today, I believe that You are here, nourishing, sustaining, giving me abundant grace, wisdom, and strength for every good deed.

Now it's your turn. On your paper, write out a personal and specific application of the character of God. Consider what God has promised and how He will meet your inability. Make biblical "considering" a regular part of your daily time with God.

---

**Bonus:**

To help focus the mind on the character of God, I have created a set of 60 printable cards on the names and attributes of God. This free printable is a gift from me to you and can be downloaded here:
www.arabahjoy.com/trust-attributes/

---

# ~Day 10~

# Sneakers

*"Jesus said to him, 'Stand up! Pick up your mat and walk.' Immediately the man was healed, and he picked up his mat and started walking."*
**(John 5:8-9, NET)**

It's a Sunday afternoon when the storm rolls in. Jackson is catnapping on the couch amidst kids building tents and towers, and I slip into the bedroom to listen to a sermon on audio. I'm listening to Pastor John Piper on desiring God and being satisfied in Jesus, and unbeknownst to me, there is a cloud of dark hunger rolling into the room next door, this insidious secret craving.

I learn of it when she comes to me in the bedroom. "Is there anything I can do for you, Momma?" she asks innocently.

I notice her face is greasy. I let it go thinking maybe the glisten is sweat. But then she lifts her hand and I notice the greasy wrist, the slick fingertips. "Baby..." I trail off and take her hand and smell it. Yep, the unmistakable smell of sesame oil.

"Baby, have you been eating noodles?"

We had lunch two hours ago. The kids had spaghetti and Jackson and I had grabbed takeout—greasy noodles. Leftovers still sit on the table. Leftovers that Little Bit decided to help herself to when no one was looking.

The problem isn't that she helped herself; it's the secrecy. It takes me a bit to get over the shock. This is a new thing for her, although not uncommon for adopted children from hard places. The first time it happened was two weeks ago and involved breakfast. I was in the bedroom when she got up. With no one else awake, she saw her chance to binge. She took it then and now she's done it again. With the other kids in the tent and Jackson and I not paying attention, she helped herself to the open food on the table.

I'm broken-hearted that in the moment of opportunity, my Little Bit is compelled to sneak—*when everything here is hers already.*

Hunger is normal. It happens to us several times every day. There is nothing wrong with eating and having our cravings satisfied. But we are to eat before the Lord,[25] who gives all things for our enjoyment. We are to eat in open acknowledgement of His generosity and joy at our wellbeing. We are to eat in humble gratitude and joyful, trusting dependence upon Him. Be it food or sex or fame or power or a thousand other good things, we are to partake of them with the Lord's blessing, and never apart from it.

Sneaking is dangerous ground. Guilty pleasures are stolen goods, going outside of relationship to get what we need. It is turning away from trust and gravitating towards self-reliance. Going outside of healthy dependence on God and others means we have moved from the healthy tension of trust to an unhealthy stronghold. **We can meet legitimate needs in illegitimate ways.**

This story sounds vaguely familiar. Scenes flash through my mind of the tempter pulling this trick on our Savior: "Look, you're hungry! You feel that craving for satisfaction? Why don't you just turn these stones into

---

[25] Deuteronomy 12:7, 14:23, and 1 Timothy 6:17

bread? Everyone needs food! And besides, it would be so easy... just say the word and your needs are met."

The first temptation of Christ was the temptation to step outside of God's plan and provision, to take matters into His own hands, to sneak. It is our temptation as well. Instead of turning *to* God and trusting the Faithful Father to meet the need, we turn to self-gratification. It sounds so reasonable, so smart.

I see it on Little Bit's grease-streaked face, the fear that if she asks me for food, if she places her trust in someone other than herself, I may say no. She may have to languish in hunger. It's the fear we all have.

The first and greatest battle is always the battle to believe. Our Savior, He passed the test. He refused the easy way out and He remained in that hunger for a bit longer. How? Only trust in a generous, gracious, wise Father can do that. Christ knew delayed satisfaction made in trust was safer than stepping outside of relationship to get His need met prematurely.

Martin Luther said, *"Faith honors him whom it trusts with the most reverent and highest regard since it considers him truthful and trustworthy. There is no honor equal to the estimate of truthfulness and righteousness with which we honor him whom we trust. On the other hand, there is no way in which we can show greater contempt for a man than to regard him as false and wicked and to be suspicious of him, as we do when we do not trust him."*[26]

In the wilderness of testing, our Savior demonstrated to us that our God is trustworthy. Christ's entire life beckons us to commit ourselves in faith to God. He leads us in the way of faith, teaching us that it is safe to trust the Father

---

[26] Luther, Martin. As quoted in "Battling Unbelief," a message by Dr. John Piper. *www.DesiringGod.org.* Accessed September 7, 2014, <www.desiringgod.org/sermons/battling-unbelief-at-bethlehem>

with our deepest cravings. That hunger pang that feels like it is going to overwhelm? It is safe with God. The craving for approval, the need for righteousness, the longing for intimacy, the hunger for purpose—there is no shame in these things. There's just an open invitation to turn to our Father in trust.

And at the end of the test, there is nourishment: food and care at the hands of angels.[27]

---

[27] Mark 1:13

# ~Day 11~

# The One "Must-Have"

### *"In him was life, and that life was the light of all mankind."*
### (John 1:4, NIV)

Horns honk and buses emit poisonous fumes into the already polluted air. I hustle two children into the back of the taxi and we fight traffic all the way into town, cars backed up in ways possible only for a city home to ten million people. After an hour and a half in the bouncing, swerving taxi, we finally arrive at the doctor's office.

The young doctor calls us back and I explain to him why we are here. Little Bit has only grown two centimeters in the last nine months. At almost six years old, she should be sprouting like a root, growing like a weed. She isn't. Her growth has plateaued and prior tests say she's got the bone age of a three-year-old. She's not producing a growth hormone called IGF-1.

"We just really need to know what's going on," I tell the doctor. What is behind this stunted growth? Is it genetic? Neurological? Biological? And do we treat it with synthetic hormones?

The nagging question looms. *How can we get her to grow?*

The doctor orders more tests. "This is complicated and there aren't easy answers," he tells me. *In other words, this may be a very long journey.*

We get home from the doctor and hang up jackets. I'm tired and the shadows fall. The day is mostly gone and it is time for me to start dinner. I wonder if I'm making the most of my time, my life. Shuttling in taxis, sorting socks, checking homework, sharing Christ however I can. *Am I really making a difference?*

My thoughts turn dark. At this point in my Christian life, I should have more spiritual authority in my life, I reason. I should carry a sense of spiritual blessing, spilling over onto others who pass my way. What with so many lost and dying around me, and me having Living Water. I think about how in my own home, I should be much slower to anger. My words should more often be a fountain of grace and life. My vision should be much greater. My faith more compelling, more transferable.

It strikes me like an unwanted chord. Could it be that I'm a spiritual Little Bit? Have I plateaued? My spiritual growth is stunted, and what is behind it?

I throw ingredients together in the Dutch oven and while the soup simmers and the bread bakes, I open a book. Between stirring the soup and setting the table, I read words. The book was randomly selected, so the words I read from Andrew Murray in *The Master's Indwelling* astonish me:

> *I speak to you as babes in Christ.*[28]

___
[28] 1 Corinthians 3:1-2

*We find in the Corinthians simply a condition of protracted infancy. It is quite right that at six months of age a babe should eat nothing but milk, but years have passed by and it remains in the same weakly state. Now this is just the condition of many believers. We come in contact with them and there is none of the beauty of holiness or of the power of God's spirit in them.*

*"You have had the gospel so long that by this time you ought to be teachers, and yet you need that men should teach you..." (Hebrews 5:12).[29]*

Soup simmers and children play while the words find their target in me. The Word becomes the physician, pinpointing the problem, giving a reason for my protracted infancy: "You've had the gospel...yet..."

For many years I've possessed what Paul describes as "the power of God." **It is no impotent thing.** Yet how skilled am I at wielding it in daily life? Does it lay unused and unapplied in the mess and the mundane? Is it really the *power* of God, say, for my speech? My witness? My vision and faith? My parenting? Is the gospel taken up— ingested—to the nourishment and growth of soul bones?

Or is Pinterest more practical to me than the gospel?

Can I really say the gospel is the power of God in my every day, moment-to-moment living? Or have I relegated the gospel as beneficial primarily for the lost?

---

[29] Murray, Andrew. *The Master's Indwelling*, Public Domain

I stagger at the implications. *Do I even know what I'm doing?*

When did I revert to the subtle ways of duty-living the Christian life instead of gospel-living it? When did my approach to the Christian life become a stack of Christian how-to books on the bedside table? An endless list of opinions and workbooks and should do's and to do's and empty guarantees?

The Word rises in my heart again and I remember. Words spoken by Peter, one who grew in spurts and plateaus and flat-on-face falls. Yes, give me Peter. "Grow in grace..." he instructed his readers.[30]

And burly Peter takes me aside and speaks it plain. "It's like this," I can hear him say. **"*Grace* equals growth."** I admit it means something coming from one who knew a thing or two about the ups and downs, the ins and outs, the failures and successes of walking the Christ life.

Is not our struggling to live the Christian life really this, the struggle to embrace grace[31] in its moment by moment delivery?

The world can only relate to us in terms of the law, a system of earning and securing. It's a system of working and achieving and proving our worth. It's the way employers relate with employees and parents relate with children and the government with its citizens. Sadly, it is frequently how we function in the church, as believing

---

[30] 2 Peter 3:18
[31] Hebrews 12:15

people. But should this really, rightly, be the believer's modus operandi?

God offers an entirely different system of relating. He offers grace.

While the world presses us to relate according to its terms and conditions, God says it simply. "Grow in Grace." Grow by grace. Grow through grace. This is the gospel. The gospel is, in fact, the grace of God.[32] And for this, we never outgrow our desperate, pressing need for daily grace.

As long as our approach to living the Christian life is a stack of how-to books on the bedside table, a study of Christian should's and to do's, a Pinterest board of Christianized ideas to try, we will never see the growth we desire, the growth we know is possible.

Grace = Growth. Thank you very much, Peter.

I'm thinking my life needs a new orientation, the orientation of grace. It's the way to spiritual growth, this trusting in grace. And what better day to start growing than today?

---

[32] Acts 20:24

*TRUST without BORDERS*

# ~Day 12~

# From Here to There

**"The thief comes only to steal
and kill and destroy;
I came that they may have life,
and have it abundantly."
(John 10:10)**

When she reached for the bottle, how could she have known where it would take her? Who would have known that one little decision would dump her like a used-up woman at the curb after dark? Destitute and alone, she only wishes she could go back and do it all over. She'd say, "No, thanks," when the bottle was passed and hand that thing right back. *Life would be alright again.*

And when he signed off on that fraudulent expense, who would have known the heartache he opened himself up to? He sold his very soul and sacrificed his family in the process. Now he watches as his son heads down the same destructive path. *If only he had known then what he knows now…*

And when that mom with three children drove down a dusky Georgia highway at 8 p.m. and decided to answer a text, how was she to know that she had just made the worst decision of her life? Now she's responsible for the death of a young woman named Marcy, an eighteen-year-old girl whose momma now moans at night. It happened so fast, sweet Marcy never saw the van cross that dotted middle line.

If things weren't bad enough for that mom of three—some people in her town call her a murderer—she has to live each second of every day and night with the reality of her own loss. She's not a mom of three anymore. She took two other lives that night, her two-year-old dinosaur-loving little boy and her five-year-old princess.

What she wouldn't do to turn back the clock, to have those precious children bickering in the backseat of the van again. She'd throw that stupid phone out the window.

Her oldest, their firstborn, lies in critical condition. She waits, heart stunned by grief, as time ticks. Each second shaves away at her sliver-thin hope. How will she be able to pull the plug on him, too?

All for a text.

Grief and remorse are almost too much to bear. *Yet who is exempt from them?* And when I pray for mommas who've whispered regret over bad choices in life, and for my own regrets, I'm not quite sure what to say. Not quite sure how to pray. I only know *how it feels* to regret something so bad, to have lost something so precious, and to know you can't ever go back.

One morning I'm reading while the crickets still chirp and the dark lays heavy outside, my children tucked safely in their beds. I'm in Jeremiah and God's people have made terrible choices. There is nothing new under the sun and all temptations are common to man and God knows we are all but dust, the same frail sinners since the Garden.

In Jeremiah, God's people are paying dearly for their choices. Their little boys stagger under heavy loads, racked with hunger, their skin shriveled on their bones. The Israelites are so desperate, the mommas even eat their own offspring. These are a people suffering because of their poor choices. They ask Jeremiah to call on God. *Where else can you go?*

Jeremiah waits to hear what God will say.

Maybe He'll tell them, "You should have known better." Or maybe He will say, "I told you this would happen! I warned you and warned you and you wouldn't listen!" or, "You brought this on yourself. Now deal with it!" What will He say?

Jeremiah waits 10 days for an answer from God. Then it comes: "This is what the LORD, the God of Israel says, 'If you stay in this land, I will build you up and not tear you down.'"

*What? Come again?*

"I will plant you and not uproot you, for I am grieved over the disaster I have inflicted on you. Do not be afraid..."[33]

God's answer comes from His nature, His character, the essence of who He is: "I will show you compassion and restore you to your land." It seems too good to be true. Really? After all the bad choices, the outright rebellion? After we've sacrificed our own children and turned into addicts and sown our wild seeds that we're now reaping? There is still hope for us? How can this be?

---

[33] Read the entire account in Jeremiah 41 and 42

It really is unbelievable, this thing we call grace.

Grace is the outflow of a Person and He will not, He cannot, change.

**But there is one catch. God asks us to trust Him.** God knew His people, the Israelites, were tempted to take matters into their own hands. They were tempted to think that since they had gotten themselves into this mess, surely they couldn't expect God to fix it. It's our thinking, too. We've got to lie down and suffer on the bed we've made. We've got to find the next best solution.

But God says to trust Him for a miracle – not the miracle of bringing the child back from the dead, or the miracle of eliminating sin's consequences, or the miracle of a movie-like life, of waking up on Groundhog Day again and again until we live it right. No, He asks us to trust for the miracle of something perhaps even greater: joy, peace, fullness, and fruitfulness *anyway*. *In the midst of it. "If you stay in this land..."*

God says, "Don't take matters into your own hands. Do not go to Egypt. Stay right where you're at."[34] Egypt was a refuge. It offered food, protection, survival. It looked like the only way out of their mess. But God said, "Don't take the way out. *Trust Me*."

And so I pray for that momma who is labeled a reckless murderer, that she won't take the way out through suicide, or divorce, or the bottle, or pills. I pray she turns to HIM. I pray for those mommas who sob quiet, the ones up late at night, filled with heartache. I pray they don't take the easy

---

[34] Jeremiah 42:7-17

way out, go down to Egypt, concoct some plan. I pray they turn open-handed and desperate to Him.

The question of greatest importance is never, "How can I go back?" When we've royally blown it, when we've devastated the landscape of our lives and families, the vital question is *"How will I go forward? Will I still choose to trust God in the midst of my failure?"*

Will we trust that His goodness truly is greater than our sin and its effects?

Lamentations 3:22-23 says it straight out, that His compassions are both present and powerful. They are new every morning, always fresh-brewed for us each day. The literal meaning of the word "great" in this verse is "powerful and strong." Our God's faithfulness is power on our behalf! Why do we languish when we have so great a salvation? He will not remove His compassions from us and His mercies are not without effect!

**"This is what you are saying, Israel, 'Our offenses and sins weigh us down, and we are wasting away because of them. How then can we live?' 'As surely as the Lord lives,' declares the *Sovereign Lord, 'I take no pleasure in the death of the wicked, but rather that they turn from their ways and live.'"* (Ezekiel 33:10)**

We can't change our choices of the past. What we can do is choose—right now—to trust God. We can throw ourselves fully upon His mercy and on His good character, knowing that he who trust in the Lord will never be disappointed.

# ~Day 13~

# Two Lambs

**"I am the good shepherd, and I know My own and My own know Me, even as the Father knows Me and I know the Father; and I lay down My life for the sheep. I have other sheep, which are not of this fold; I must bring them also, and they will hear My voice ..."**
**(John 10:14-16a)**

She toddles out of her room carrying a brown elephant by its trunk. "Good morning, Sunshine," I greet her. We exchange hugs and slobbery kisses and tickled laughs. Then I ask where her sister is.

"She won't come out."

I sigh. Here we go again. In the providence of God, I have two daughters the same age. One is healthy and attached. The other is not. One climbs in my lap unhindered and calls me in the night without hesitation. She knows what it is like to feel safe, to trust. To laugh free and share deep. To belong.

The other? Not so much. She is scarred. Unattached. She came to us after a very long and hard first year of life. She carries memories deep and trust is a risk she can't afford. To her, safety is in controlling, not in running to her momma and daddy and throwing herself headlong upon us.

My two daughters have brought a rich depth to my understanding of God. Both daughters are fully mine. They both eat the same things, have the same resources, share the same last name. They swap clothes, toys, and hold the same citizenship, despite their different genetic makeup, backgrounds, and pasts. They both have all of me and my resources at their disposal.

The only difference is that one unquestioningly knows it and the other is plagued with doubt and distrust.

I've asked it many times: Which daughter am I? Am I the daughter that has laid hold[35] of all that has been freely given her? Or am I the daughter that still stumbles and falters?

It does strike me then, after all the times I have done this, after all the mornings Little Bit has resisted, withdrawn, and outright refused. After all the times her doubt and distrust has put her in a bad spot, leaving me to coax her out of her self-imposed prison, it finally dawns on me. *I am like the Shepherd.* The Shepherd leaves the 99 healthy sheep in the fold to go after the single, solitary one who is lost.

I've been invited to enter into His very heart, to reach out the finger, to touch His wounded side that speaks of the distance He went. I'm invited to **believe**. I've been the wounded daughter, the lost sheep, the doubting Thomas. I'm the black sheep on the outside looking in.

And to experience His heart, to touch His side, to no longer doubt but believe, He has given me two little lambs.

---

[35] This powerful little phrase is used by Paul in Philippians 3:12

Parenting allows us to see firsthand how He shepherds His own. Our Shepherd is One who goes after the wounded and sick, the needy one stuck in some pit on the backside of nowhere.

His intent is nothing short of *bringing in*.[36] He will keep pursuing, keep reaching, keep leading, until each of His sheep are all *brought in:* safe, attached, tended, and looked after fully in His fold.

My sigh turns to a smile. As much as I'd love to cuddle with my healthy little lamb, I leave her sitting on the couch in order to bring in my lost one. "Little Bit," I beckon her from the foot of her bed. "Are you ready to get up?"

She doesn't respond. She is rigid and her eyes glint at me hard. She isn't budging. "We are having breakfast in a little while and you are invited to join us."

She starts to cry. She has placed herself in a predicament, you see. She wants breakfast. But she doesn't want to reach out. She doesn't want to be dependent upon anyone. She's decided she doesn't care much for the offer I've made her, to be part of the family, to belong, to give and take. I see it in her rigid body. She knows it's easier to stay stuck than to reach out.

The truth is sordid sometimes: being a victim is easier than embracing grace. I'm like my Little Bit and I see clearly, the moments dotting my day, impurities pocking a life, times where I don't want to stretch into the grace offered me. I want something easier. I want to live

---

[36] I love that one of the Shepherd's intent is to "bring in," according to John 10:16

closed-fisted, demanding change from others, from life itself. I'm unwilling to embrace the change God gently prompts within.

The ugly truth is that I often don't want the challenge of grace. So I stay stuck.

But hunger for that breakfast table has a way of doing a work. And the Shepherd has a way of making us desperately hungry for Grace.

I lean against the bunk beds shared by my lambs. I look at Little Bit. She wants control and I give it. "Alright, just come on out when you are ready."

I leave the room and wait. One of two things will happen. I know because we have done this little routine numerous times. She will either start screaming, hoping to elicit a response from me, or she will slowly inch her way out of the bed, take baby steps towards the door, and finally make a very reserved, staunch, proud appearance.

Today she does neither.

This time, I hear her voice amidst the cries, amidst the tears. ***"Momma, I need help!"***

**I *run*.** I reach her side and lift her up. I hold that Little Bit of a girl, telling her I am right there and it's what I'm here for, to help her, and that I will always help her when she asks. I hear the Shepherd's voice in my ear, speaking to me the very words I speak to her.

"That's the promise I've made you," I whisper into her tear-soaked hair. "And I will always keep it. Always."

I think of the Shepherd who made a covenant *with His very own blood* and how He promises to never leave us or forsake us, to always be faithful because He cannot deny His nature. Even when we can't help ourselves, when we can't reach out, when we flounder in doubt, when we want grace but don't have the strength to embrace it, all we need to do is call out and He is there. He will bring us in.

I lift up my Little Bit, soothe her tears, and carry her on the hip. I bring her into the fold. We join the rest of the family at the breakfast table. Little Bit shudders a breath as I lower her into her chair. I trumpet it like a victor: "Let's eat!"

And all hands reach out, a circle of fists holding hands, grabbing grace—lavish grace broken and poured out. The family is complete. We've all come in and in the quiet pastures of the soul, I feel the Shepherd smiling. **Grace has won.**

*TRUST without BORDERS*

# ~Day 14~

# **Wilderness**

***"Jesus then said to them,***
***'Truly, truly, I say to you,***
***it was not Moses who gave you the bread***
***from heaven, but my Father gives you***
***the true bread from heaven.'"***
**(John 6:32, ESV)**

"My father used to beat me," he says. "It's really the only thing I remember from my childhood—*the fear.* My Daddy ..." his voice falters, comes back bitter. "I'd beg him to stop. 'Please, *Daddy, please,* no more.' But he wouldn't listen."

I see the tears, feel the desperation of that small child, and I gulp back the ache in my throat.

"I've struggled with fear my whole life," Mr. Clinton says it, this missionary man, father, fellow broken one.

Yes, broken ones know fear.

And for all I'm worth, all I can think about are those Israelites. They left Egypt wounded, weary from oppression. Broken. They'd jumped to the commands of others their whole lives, driven by fear. They had the scars to prove it.

Sure, after 400 years they finally had their freedom, and sure, they had a Shepherd to go before them. But they were accustomed to slavery. They had grown up looking over shoulders. All they'd known was the whip. How do you live free when you've never had freedom? How do you stop fearing when fear is all you've ever known?

And for this predicament, God does the strangest thing. He takes this broken people aside and introduces Himself as Yahweh-Rapha, the God who heals.[37] So far, so good, right? But then He leads them straight into deep deprivation. First, no food. Then, no water. Then, He allows the weakest of them to be attacked from behind in an unexpected onslaught.[38] They are a weak, wounded, untrained, abused people—not warriors. Not miracle workers.

*And this is how Rapha God brings healing?*

"These last few months have nearly killed me," Mr. Clinton says flatly. "My oldest son has embraced an alternative lifestyle. One of my daughters was expelled from school for smoking and drinking. Someone anonymously called our mission agency to report supposed sexual abuse on my part towards my daughters. I've had attorneys and investigations and suspicions … all of them completely unfounded."

Then Mr. Clinton says something I never would have dreamed. "You know what all this has done?" he asks. "It's made me face my fears."

Mr. Clinton has known the deprivation of the wilderness. He's thirsted for relief. He's wondered where sustenance

---

[37] Exodus 15:22-27
[38] Exodus 16-17

will come from. He's been attacked from behind. Mr. Clinton, he's learned what someone else stated so well: "The mattering part is never what *isn't.*" Circumstances aren't what matters *most.* What matters is always what *is,* and God forever is I AM. Life can give us the bread of adversity and Moses can pray for some manna, but Jesus? Jesus is real food.

Like the Israelites, Mr. Clinton has learned it doesn't really matter if your greatest fears come true. Because no matter what, I AM is always Enough. ***Really.***

I AM is the Bread[39] when you hunger and your belly aches.

I AM is the Rock[40] when the world spins crazy.

I AM is the Water[41] in the dryness.

I AM is the shelter[42] from the scorching heat.

I AM is the blanket of comfort.[43]

I AM is the Warrior[44] who covers in victory.

For each and every need, **I AM is enough**.

---

[39] John 6:35
[40] Acts 4:10-12
[41] John 7:38
[42] Psalm 121:5-6
[43] 2 Corinthians 1:3-5
[44] Exodus 17:8-16

And could it be that the wilderness is the Shepherd's way of teaching us real freedom? Because when we have I AM, we have it all.

*Who would have thought?* Perhaps this is why we run from the wilderness instead of embrace it. We don't realize how Rapha God heals. We don't understand how He removes the Egypt from us. We think He's driving *us* but He's really driving *out* fear.

Mr. Clinton, he tells us he's starting over. He's moving out west, out to the middle of nowhere. He'll be living in a small home his brother has. He doesn't have possessions, he's lost his reputation, he doesn't have a job lined up, and he sure doesn't know what the future holds. Sadly enough, he doesn't have children with their faith intact.

But he's not afraid anymore. The wilderness has trained him to rely solely on His God. And He does not disappoint.[45]

I look at Mr. Clinton and I do believe that's water from the Jordan clinging to his clothes. He has crossed over from wilderness wandering into the blessed land of abundance. He has learned how to dig deep into Jesus and find in Him all he needs. No matter what. Yes. This is the portion of the broken. If only we will trust.

---

[45] Isaiah 49:23

"Remember how the Lord your God led you through the wilderness for these forty years, humbling you and testing you. Yes, he humbled you by letting you go hungry and then feeding you with manna, a food previously unknown to you and your ancestors. He did it to teach you that people do not live by bread alone; rather, we live by every word that comes from the mouth of the Lord. Think about it: Just as a parent disciplines a child, the Lord your God disciplines you for your own good."

(Deuteronomy 8:2-5)

# ~Day 15~

# Faith Living

*"The Word became flesh and made his
dwelling among us. We have seen his glory,
the glory of the one and only Son,
who came from the Father,
full of grace and truth."*
**(John 1:14, NIV)**

It's one of those days. I wake up to the boys bickering, to yesterday's unfolded laundry, to our emotionally troubled child having a meltdown, and all four children wanting breakfast. I feel it creeping in, the feelings of being over-whelmed, sucked plumb dry before the day even gets started. I know I'm inadequate for this job of juggling and training and nurturing and soothing and educating. I feel the fear.

I'm like Sarah again, that mother of *nations*, standing in the shadows. She simply laughed at the likelihood of her calling, as if she was capable of birthing even a single child at such a ripe, old age.

Yes, sometimes God calls us mothers to the right impossible.

Today's mom expresses Sarah-like unbelief through, perhaps, excessive internet surfing. Or perhaps through avoiding responsibility. Or with busyness, shopping, or even hard work, striving like Abraham and Sarah to fulfill

God's promises *for Him.* But at the core, in the shadows of the heart, there is unbelief in God.

Eventually, we must allow the impossibility of our calling to lead us out of the shadows and into the exercise of faith. We must follow in the steps of Sarah, from beginning to end.

Faith is how the impossible takes on flesh and becomes tangible. It's how the dead places inside us are brought to life.[46] It's how we face the bickering children with a soothing word, how we walk an anxious child through a meltdown, how we meet tension and demands with a playful laugh instead of a harsh word, how we roll out of bed with a smile instead of a groan (yes, even before we have our coffee!).

Faith is forged in daily life. Trust is for the real world, not some Sunday-only ideal. Faith is how God's Word, His promises for our children and future, takes on flesh and dwells amongst us.

Our days are full of opportunity for faith. From the moment I swing my feet onto the floor I have a choice, to stumble through the morning as best I can or to step out in faith, believing God is with me. He is giving me an abundance of grace for every need. I can push my children away, or I can draw them close and sing as we ask God to fill us. I can retreat from the demands or, by faith, I can soothe raw emotions and lean on Jesus to give me heart, strength, love, and grace. Faith is how I can see miraculous conception of the divine in this barren womb of a day.

---

[46] Hebrews 11:11

God has called us to the impossible and we have to trust Him to make it happen in real, practical, tangible ways. His ways give birth to flesh, to Isaac, to the fulfillment of promise in daily living.

After a day of faith-living, a small one climbs onto my lap and whispers in my ear, *"I see Jesus in you, Momma."* Isn't this what mothering is all about? Allowing Jesus to incarnate Himself in us? Seeing the Word take on flesh for eyes to behold?

This confidence called faith does indeed have great reward. Brothers and sisters, let us not throw it away![47]

---

[47] Hebrews 10:35

# ~Day 16~

# A Letter to My Daughter

**"For not even his brothers
were believing in him."
(John 7:5)**

**Dear Daughter,**

When they told me what we had to do, the world stopped and I just needed to pull you close and sit down. They said in order for you to grow, I must give you injections every night before bed. But that isn't the worst part. "They'll need to be given in the stomach," the doctors told me, "and will continue until she has reached adult height, in about *ten years.*"

And I don't know what the next ten years will bring us, but I know **hard things and painful nights will certainly be part of our lives.** I wish there were some other way, a way to avoid pain and discomfort. In this life, there is no such way.

That's why it is important for me to give you something greater than a pain-free life, my daughter. I want to impart to you *perspective.*

I want to train you how to see the unseen. So daughter, I'm shopping for a teacup. Yes, you and I are going to sit down to tea. Before the injections start in a few days and our evenings shift and change, you and I are going to have tea. **And I'm going to tell you a story ...**

## The Teacup Story

*Once upon a time there was a quiet little shop tucked away amongst the busy streets of London. This shop was magic because from time to time, items in the shop, items like wooden horses and over-stuffed elephants, would briefly come to life. One day a little girl and her mother were visiting London and got lost. They stumbled into the quiet little shop and began looking at the varied items found there.*

*The mom noticed high on a shelf sat a beautiful teacup. It was lovely! The mother reached for the cup to show her daughter. As they touched the delicate flowers and ran fingers across the cup's rim, something surprising happened. The cup began to speak!*

***"I have not always been a teacup.*** *You see, there was a time when I was just a lump of clay. My master took me and rolled me, patted and pounded me over and over and I yelled out, 'Don't do that. I don't like it! Leave me alone.' But he only smiled, and gently said, 'Not yet!'*

*Then WHAM! I was placed on a spinning wheel and suddenly I was spun around and around and around. 'Stop it! I'm getting so dizzy! I'm going to be sick,' I screamed. But the master only nodded and said, quietly, 'Not yet.'*

*He spun me and poked and prodded and bent me out of shape to suit himself and then… then he put me in the oven. I never felt such heat. I yelled and knocked and pounded at the door. 'Help! Get me out of here!' I could see him through the opening and I could read his lips as he shook his head from side to side, 'Not yet.'*

**When I thought I couldn't bear it another minute**, *the door opened. He carefully took me out and put me on the shelf, and I began to cool. Oh, that felt so good! Ah, this is much better, I thought. But, after I cooled he picked me up and he brushed and painted me all over. The fumes were horrible. I thought I would gag. 'Oh, please, stop it! Stop it!' I cried. He only shook his head and said, 'Not yet!'*

*Then suddenly he put me back into the oven. Only it was not like the first one. This was twice as hot and I just knew I would suffocate. I begged. I pleaded. I screamed. I cried. I was convinced I would never make it. I was ready to give up. Just then the door opened and he took me out and again placed me on the shelf, where I cooled and waited—and waited, wondering "What's he going to do to me next?*

*An hour later he handed me a mirror and said* **'Look at yourself.'** *And I did. I said, 'That's* **not me, that couldn't be me. It's beautiful. I'm beautiful!'**

*Quietly he spoke, 'I want you to remember. I know it hurt to be rolled and pounded and patted, but had I just left you alone, you'd have dried up.*

*I know it made you dizzy to spin around on the wheel, but if I had stopped, you would have crumbled.*

*I know it hurt and it was hot and disagreeable in the oven, but if I hadn't put you there, you would have cracked.*

*I know the fumes were bad when I brushed and painted you all over, but if I hadn't done that, you never would have hardened. You would not have had any color in your life. If I hadn't put you back in that second oven, you wouldn't have survived for long because the hardness would not have held. Now you are a finished product.* **Now you are what I had in mind when I first began with you.'**[48]

Daughter, you are like that teacup. God is the Potter of your life. His plan and delight is to make something stunningly beautiful of you. But beauty doesn't just happen. **Beauty is shaped with intentionality.** In fact, beauty and purpose sometimes only come with force, fire, and discomfort.

---

[48] This rendition of the teacup story is my own. The author of the original story is unknown.

If our teacups could talk to us right now, they would tell us it was all worth it. The shaping and the fumes, the fire and the heat. One day, you will be able to say the same thing.

**For now, we must get to know our Potter. He is good, always... and always faithful. He knows what He's doing.** In wisdom, He knows just what to bring into our lives to shape the beauty, color, and flavor He aims for us to have. He never takes His eyes from you or forgets what you are going through. He never gets tired of His project or decides to quit. He promises to finish what He started in you.[49] He even wrote you a letter so you can know for sure and never forget:

**"For I know the plans I have for you, declares the Lord, plans to prosper you and not to harm you, plans to give you a hope and a future." (Jeremiah 29:11, ESV)**

Oh daughter! I can see the beauty taking shape in you! I can see determination starting to shine through. I can see gentleness being formed. I even catch glimpses of compassion and service. Daughter, you are a master-piece. Whenever you are tempted to despair, whenever you are tossed about with doubt, this will be our tradition ... we'll pull out the teacups and reflect on our Potter.

Much love, Momma

---

[49] Philippians 1:6

*TRUST without BORDERS*

# ~Day 17~

# No Limits

*"As He passed by,*
*He saw a man blind from birth.*
*And His disciples asked Him, 'Rabbi,*
*who sinned, this man or his parents,*
*that he would be born blind?' Jesus answered,*
*'It was neither that this man sinned,*
*nor his parents; but it was so that the works*
*of God might be displayed in him.'"*
**(John 9:1-3)**

"Everyone longs to believe two things. One, that you are loved. Two, that everything is going to be okay. I wanted to believe that everything was going to be okay...but how could it be?"

This comes from Nick Vujicic, a man who has known difficulty. As a little boy, Nick wondered how he could trust a God who didn't give him limbs. No arms. No legs. No normal life. Nick would go to Sunday School and read Jeremiah 29:11, *you know, the verse that says the Lord's plans are good?* And Nick would think, "That might be true for other people, but it isn't true for me. Look at everything I can't do."

And one wonders, how does a person move from that place of despondency and doubt to writing a book not titled "*Life Without Limbs*" but "*Life Without Limits?*"

An interviewer asked Nick the question: "So what was the turning point for you?"

And Nick said there came a time at 15 years of age when he chose to trust. "It was when I read John 9. It is the story of Jesus healing the blind man and I realized that *God knows* what He is doing. God understands. God, who is bigger than my circumstance, is letting this happen for a reason. I prayed... 'God, I don't understand this circumstance, but I trust *You*.'" Nick then shared the path he walked to trust. "The gospel of John has changed my life."

No matter where we are, no matter how far we have fallen, no matter the pit we are in, regardless of how beaten down and worn out, how despondent, how full of doubt we are, we can begin to trust by taking in scripture.

**"These things were written so that you might believe and in believing, you may have life in His name."**
**(John 20:31)**

For today, I invite you to click over and view the 15-minute interview with Nick. You can find it here: http://arabahjoy.com/trust-Nick/

I also challenge you to begin reading through the book of John a chapter at a time. Perhaps at night before bed? As you read, ask these three questions:

## Faith-Building Interaction with the Text:

1. What does this passage say about the character of God?

2. Based on this, why should I trust God?

3. If this is really true about God's nature, how should my life look? i.e. What would my life look like if I decided to trust that God is who He says and represents Himself to be?

# ~Day 18~

# Linda's Cross

**"His disciples did not understand these things at first, but when Jesus was glorified, then they remembered that these things had been written about him and had been done to him."**
**(John 12:16, ESV)**

It's a sticky July morning when we pile into the van and follow country roads to their house. We pass the bank on the hill and the digital sign blinks 99 degrees. *Already?*

Mr. Ian greets us when we arrive. "My, my, you've got your hands full," he says, referencing the four little ones who seem to have turned into squirrels upon entering their home. They are going from window to window, pressing faces against panes to see the many species of birds, the fish in the fountain, the hibiscus bathed in delicate peach.

"Let children be children," Mr. Ian says as we fret about the prints we are leaving behind. Mr. Ian's the one who does all the cleaning. "Linda will be down shortly," he says, then gives us an update. "She looks better than she is. By looking at her you wouldn't know anything is wrong. But when I cut her eggs in the mornings ..." Mr. Ian trails off.

My heart goes soft at this man who stoops low to carry another, who cooks special meals, cleans up sickness, and cuts eggs.

"Her hands and feet are blistered, fingers numb. The doctors say there's nothing more they can do, so we'll just keep taking the meds."

Ms. Linda does look good when she comes down. You wouldn't know her liver is full of hot spots and under her left arm there's a lump. Jackson takes the children for a look at the wonders outside while I talk with these two precious ones. She tells me it's been five years and the meds she's on now are better than the ones before but that's enough about her.

"How are you?" she asks.

I choke back the tears. I don't want to talk about me. I want to go to my knees and serve them really the only way I can, with beseeching prayer. I struggle through the questions, trying to tell them what we are doing, where we are headed in a few weeks. Then Jackson returns and the four of us huddle around the sofa on our knees. We've somehow made a circle, our hands and hearts entwined.

As we pray, Ms. Linda says it soft, "Yes, Jesus," and Mr. Ian is heaving big sobs, a broken man drawing water from the Well. It's the Spirit who intercedes and Joshua 1 is what He's pressing on our hearts, out of our lips. "Every place on which the sole of your foot treads, *I have given it to you.* From the wilderness to the setting of the sun will be your territory."[50]

I see Linda's blistered feet beside me – red, swollen, and painful from the journey through her wilderness. Even so, I

---

[50] For a shot of encouragement, read Joshua 1:3-6

know this place she treads, though hard and rocky and painful, it is "given" to her.

*That makes it a gift.*

And it says so right there in scripture: Every *inch* is a gift, be it the glory of the sunset, the dryness of the desert, or everything in between—**every inch is gift.**

"Oh, God!" I cry out on behalf of dear ones. "Give us vision! Restore faith where it has faltered, for You have *given* this land. We don't understand, Lord, but help us believe."

When our prayers are completed, Mr. Ian just shakes silent with the burden and the blessing. He wraps arms tight around me and I know *this* is a gift. We all walk to the car and Mr. Ian looks at me, pointing at the guest house.

"You see that, girl?" he asks.

"Yes, sir," I nod back.

"That is where we meet every Friday night and call down the heavens, like we just did inside. With you all headed back overseas, He's on me to start meeting for you again."

I realize in a very real way, I might have been a small reason for this couple's cross. I see the brokenness in them, the five long years of pain and struggle, the unknowns. I see the burden they bear. Their cross caused awareness of the desperate need, a desperation which drives one to agonizing prayer.

Something niggles inside, words that need a hearing. Jesus' words, there in the Garden, when the cross was pressing close. I follow Him in my mind, go with Him into the Garden, envision Him asking His disciples to watch and pray. I hear the words He utters, "Could you not tarry with Me one hour?"[51]

Jesus asks us to tarry in prayer.

When the cross presses, it presses us to prayer which paves the way for the Kingdom of God to come in power. Voices in the wilderness always prepare the way of the Lord. This gift, this wilderness, this cross, it is the bearing, the laboring, and the unleashing of the kingdom of God. The gift is the invitation to participate in redemption.

It all converges, the nail scarred hands, the blistered feet, the tears in the Garden, the words whispered, "Not my will but Thine, Thy kingdom come." The tarrying, the invitation, the gift. The unleashing of heaven.

But how can we bear with Him if we do not believe, if we have no vision for the victory, the purpose, the glory, no vision of the redemptive story being accomplished through the cross? No vision of the rent veil, the throngs before the throne? In the bearing of our cross do we not understand how we fill up and flesh out the sufferings of Christ?[52]

Surely His people perish for lack of vision.

---

[51] Matthew 26:38-45
[52] Colossians 1:24

We return home and I stand at the sink before a pile of dirty dishes, the cry for faith on my lips, the prayer for vision of the joy set before me. The flesh is weak and eyes are prone to fail.

There at the sink He answers my prayer for faith. "You must always trust Me, because even in the desert, and you know even the wilderness is a gift, I will make a road.[53] Even in dry lands I will make rivers for you. Jump in with both feet, blistered though they are, because you can trust Me."

I look down at my feet, weary, worn, and unsure. I jump. I jump into the path before me. Both feet driven by trust.

---

[53] Isaiah 43:19

# ~Day 19~

## Stress Inoculation

***"When they were filled, He said to His disciples, 'Gather up the leftover fragments so that nothing will be lost.' So they gathered them up, and filled twelve baskets with fragments from the five barley loaves which were left over by those who had eaten."***
**(John 6:12-13)**

The sun is peaking under the shades when I finally throw the covers back and switch on the light. I groan when I see the time. 6:39 a.m. So much for a quiet time this morning. I regret turning the alarm off. I know it is a matter of mere moments before the children are up.

"Lord," I pray. "I know You are with me. I know You will help me. Thank You for breath, for legs that work, for these children that will bustle out any second. Thank You for what You're doing in my life."

I do not feel strong. Dread is creeping into my heart. Jackson is out of town and the demands of the day fall squarely, solely, on me. Pondering what lies ahead of me today makes me shake in my proverbial boots.

So I become a spiritual Navy Seal.

Seals are trained for success through something called "stress inoculation." It happens by being repeatedly placed in high stress situations that trigger a panic response.

Yes, that sounds familiar. Parenting isn't for the faint of heart.

Seals are trained to keep the emotional center of the brain in check. When pushed to the breaking point, the trainee learns to override the panic response. It isn't something that comes naturally. It isn't a "zap" that happens while they sleep one night. It happens through repeated training.

Scriptures refer to the Christian as a warrior, a soldier in training. We must know how to effectively deal with pressure, difficulty, and high stress situations. We are instructed to put on the full armor and apply our training and meet each challenge standing.[54]

I go to battle.

"Lord, we will make it through breakfast," I say as I pull on pants. To combat mental chaos and suppress the negative emotions that fear evokes, Seals are pushed to the limits and required to employ four special tools. These enable the Seal to deal with the harsh realities those limits evoke. Goal-setting in small segments is one of the four techniques Seals use to train their brain.

I practice the four tips, too. I visualize how the Lord is equipping me to master the morning until breakfast. In my ten second visualization, for there is no time for lengthy ones, I see myself drawing from Jesus and responding with a smile through breakfast.

The Bible calls it renewing the mind.

---

[54] Ephesians 6:10-18

Two children exit their rooms as I exit mine. The game is on.

This is where the theory of faith is put into practice. Stress inoculation doesn't happen in a classroom. Neither does faith. **God wants our *theology* to become our methodology.** Methodology means we step out of the classroom, out from the church pew, out from the peaceful quiet of our morning time, and we enter the real, gritty, scary mess of the world.

We can attend Bible studies and conferences, hang out with friends and drink coffee, but truth is, stress inoculation happens when you're submerged under the water. And this morning, I'm submerged. Little Bit decides she does not want to get up. She refuses to come to breakfast. I leave her in bed and go take care of the other children. As I pour cereal into bowls, Little Bit begins screaming in the next room.

Two children start bickering. I run out of milk. Youngest child complains. The screaming next door escalates. Chaos starts to creep into my mind and I fight it by speaking Scripture aloud. I sing the first hymn that comes to mind.

At breakfast, I grapple hard and ask my oldest son to read from *Jesus Calling for Kids*. The words apply, even to big kids, as he reads.

> *When it seems like absolutely everything is going wrong, trust Me. When your life feels more and more out of control, thank Me. That's not what usually pops into your mind, is it? When you've*

*missed the bus, lost your best friend, and the dog really did eat your homework—your first response is to complain. Put on the brakes! Don't do the 'natural' thing, do what is beyond natural. Do what is supernatural. Trusting and being thankful in the middle of a really bad day are supernatural responses, and they unlock My supernatural Power in your life. I'll see you through whatever mess you're in and fill you up with My peace, which is beyond your understanding.*[55]

I gather the children around, all except for the one still screaming, and we sit on the living room floor. We've made it through breakfast. "Okay, Lord, let's just make it to snack time." Aloud, I say to the children, "Let's practice trusting and thanking. What are some things about God that we can trust?"

The answers pop out.

"His faithfulness."

"His power."

"His love."

"His kindness."

Then we sing. I pull out one of my personal heavy hitters, a Jeremy Camp album. We sing "I Will Trust."

[55] Young, Sarah. *Jesus Calling: 365 Devotions for Kids*, Nashville, Tennessee: Tommy Nelson, 2010

There are interruptions. A thrown toy smacks a sibling in the head. A child has to be disciplined for whining when given instruction. It is not pretty or seamless or perfect, but my mind is held steady, focused on Him. Chaos does not rule. Fear does not win. Defeat doesn't mock.

Not today.

# ~Day 20~

# Nourished

**"'Do not work for the food that perishes,
but for the food that endures to eternal life,
which the Son of Man will give to you.
For on him God the Father has set his seal.'
Then they said to him, 'What must we do,
to be doing the works of God?' Jesus answered
them, 'This is the work of God, that you
believe in him whom he has sent.'"**
(John 6:27-29, ESV)

It's been five weeks since she stopped cold turkey.

The doctor says the nicotine is flushed out of her body by now, and not a minute too soon. It was killing her. But still. Still, she gets the cravings and they are harsh. Still, when she reaches that point in the road on her drive to work, she starts shaking. She's jittery and she's a wreck and she doesn't want to die but it's not just a chemical dependency she's been fighting; it's a mental and emotional one, too.

Ask me how I know self-pity, shame, and rejection can be like cigarettes. Addictive. We can be dependent upon the very toxins that pollute us, things like anger and hatred and self-loathing. We can be addicted to death.

The Israelites craved Egypt's strong onions, garlic, leek, and fish when they made their exodus. Their bodies shook and their minds twisted and their mouths watered for that which was best left behind. Yes, we can be addicted to death, but there's a way through the wilderness. There's a substitute for leeks and garlic. There's manna from Heaven.[56]

And like the Israelites, we are to gather daily, just enough for each day; we are to gather early, before the sun comes up and the opportunity is gone. We eat words and words are our miracle bread.

The Israelites gathered a day's portion and stored it, perhaps in a jar. I place my portion on index cards and carry them with me. When the pangs come and the cravings hit, when I feel I'll die if I don't have Egypt's strong drink, I pull out those cards.

"The Lord is my Shepherd," I read aloud and inhale the words, taste them. "I shall not want."[57]

With that, Bread from Heaven becomes my daily bread.

It seems neither palatable nor powerful in the moment, not after the intense and dramatic meat pots I've eaten from. Yet with every mouthful, I am nourished in ways I can't see, one more meal removed from Egypt's death pots.

We learn to let go of Egypt by replacing toxic enticements with the simple and pure Bread of Life...

... not discounting it because it carries no odor.
... not despising it because it seems boring.

---

[56] Exodus 16
[57] Psalm 23:1

... not pushing it away because it is foreign, and we don't understand it.

We gather daily and eat the Word we gather. The miraculous happens. Words become flesh, our flesh, our new self. The Word is how God takes form and dwells among us. It's been that way since the beginning, the Word speaking into existence new life, form from void. And doesn't He promise His Word will always go forth to accomplish what He intends? **It will never return empty, never be without shape.** God-Words always take on form, become flesh, create new life.[58]

So we eat Word manna as it works power inside us, shaping and forming Christ Himself within us.[59] Dare I overlook this simple faith act of eating words? Do I relegate it to only a duty or obligation? Or can I eat in faith, trusting for a nourishment and sustainment beyond my imagination?

I tuck my portion into pockets and feast all day long. What words are you eating today?

---

[58] Genesis 1:1, John 1:1, and Isaiah 55:11
[59] Galatians 4:19

## ~Day 21~

# The Beautiful Wounded

**"For God so loved the world, that he gave
his only Son, that whoever believes
in him should not perish but have eternal life."
(John 3:16, ESV)**

I notice the man when he walks through the doors. I'm placing toilet paper and laundry detergent on the conveyor belt of the local Dollar General. Before the cashier even rings me up, there he is—in line behind me. He's holding two quarts of car oil in his dark, worn hands.

I nod and smile and turn back to my cart and to the kids now bubbling all over the front area of the store.

The Father speaks to my inner place and I hear Him quiet, *"This man needs to know I love him."*

*"Okay, Lord,"* I say. I turn back to the man with sunken face and smile again. "How are you today, sir?" I ask.

"Good, good, just hot."

This is the South and it's always the weather we fall back on when we talk small. Never mind the man is shrunk up to nothing, that his lip is bleeding, that his teeth are all gone, that he is literally wasting away for all to see. No, there is only the weather to tck tck at.

Youngest keeps reaching for the toys near the register and oldest is pushing on the cart to play with Little Bit inside. I'm trying to use coupons and pay the cashier and keep the buggy from running into my heels while instructing my other daughter to put that back already.

*"Let me get out of this caldron first?"* I ask Him as I grab my sacked paper goods and round the kids up and herd everything towards the door. Sometimes it's all I can do to think straight. We get outside and I park the cart.

The man is already out the door and I try to bargain with God. *"If he comes by here on his way to the car, then I'll tell him."*

I glance around and notice he is already at his car—on the opposite side of the lot. He won't be coming my way. A lost sheep always has to be *found.* I'll have to be a shepherd and leave the fold.

For a split second I consider forgetting it, going my way and excusing myself. But I don't want to miss what God is doing, and I don't want to quench that Voice. "C'mon, kids," I round them up. "I want to go speak with this gentleman."

They listen quickly. *Grace.*

I approach the man and his van. He's got the front hood up and is pouring oil. "Sir?" I ask. "Do you need to make a phone call? I have a phone you can use."

It feels so lame, so silly, so moronic. But it's the opportunity given and I take it.

"Oh no, ma'am."

"Well are you from out of town? Is there something I can do to help?"

"I appreciate that, but no, I just need to put oil in every now and then. We live out in the Acres and we're moving today to be near my brother." I glance inside the van and notice a woman in the passenger seat, window down, asleep.

"Well sir," I turn back to him, "I just want to tell you that God loves you." I reach out my hand and place it on his frail shoulder. "God loves you."

We are strangers and I hope I'm giving dignity to the man and not taking it by being so bold as to touch him, but all I can think of is how Jesus touched the untouchables. Up close, the man's bleeding lip reminds me of the leper. Or hepatitis. And sometimes the greatest way to love is to touch.

"Yes, well ..." The man trails off and shifts on his feet. He doesn't know what to say to that.

I look back in the van again, trying to speak with the woman. She is still asleep. I am aware of the kids around my legs. "Momma, why did we come here to talk to this man?" Youngest daughter asks outright. The man is listening, probably wondering himself.

"Because God loves him and maybe he needs help and we can help him," I tell her and glance at him, too. He has finished up and is ready to go. I turn to take the kids back across the lot when I hear the voice.

"Ma'am! Ma'am!" It's a woman's voice and I turn to see her awake and sitting up. "Are you a believer, too?" she asks. Ups and yells it out the window, she does.

"Yes ma'am. I am," I say.

She does a little jig in her seat and stretches her arms out the car window. "Oh! Oh!" She is downright giddy. "I am, too! It's so good to meet another believer!"

I walk over to her and take her hands in mine. I smile into her eyes. "Oh, it's just so good to *touch* another believer," she says.

She's as frail as her husband, but she's beautiful. And witty. I know that maybe she's strung out. Or maybe she's trying to work me. Or maybe she's a little off her rocker. *But aren't the lost sheep who Jesus came for, the ones who need a Doctor?* I squeeze her hands like there's no tomorrow and we talk. She is visibly moved and I can't believe this is put on. Her husband, the man Jesus loves, is growing antsy. I've about worn out my Southern welcome.

"We've got to go, Hon," he presses her. I invite them to church tomorrow and we exchange names. She is Jan—a simple, beautiful Jan. "Well, let go of her," the man tells her. He's already in reverse with one foot on the gas and the other on the brake.

"I'm trying," she says and laughs, eyes twinkling. We give one final squeeze and release each other.

"God loves you," I tell her and she almost cries. We turn to leave as they pull away and I wonder what just happened. I buckle the children in, pull out of the parking lot. I think of the Good Samaritan and I wonder if there was a reason why he stopped to help the wounded man? Had he been wounded once himself? Did he know what it was like to be left on the side of the road for dead? Did he serve from experience?

It's been said that hurt people hurt people. The wounded always wound others. This may be true but I know something just as true—the healed heal. Those who have encountered the Great Physician are now His hands, His feet, His body.

The Healer Himself not only heals us but uses us to bind up the wounds of others. His measure of redemption includes putting us into this service of restoration.

I get on my knees and I thank Him for beautiful Jan, for marks and reminders, for nail-scarred hands that reached and touched and anointed us to do the same, **for imperfect days that remind me I'm the kind He came for. I'm the kind He redeems.**

The Beautiful Wounded.

*TRUST without BORDERS*

# ~Day 22~

# Simplicity

**"His mother said to the servants,
'Do whatever he tells you.'"**
**(John 2:5, NIV)**

The sun rises before I do. Before the laundry gets started and the eggs get scrambled, before the children bicker and the doors slam. Before it all presses in on me, the to-do list running a mile long, that one faithful witness in the sky speaks.

*His mercies are new every morn.*[60]

Every cock-crowing, dog-barking, kid-fighting, laundry-piling morning, His mercies are new. *And I could live it.* Instead of scrambling to get up and get going, to beat the clock and outrun the sun, **I could just believe that today is covered.**

It's all covered.

It's lying open there on the table when I stumble out of the bedroom. The ancient Words spoken to a fretful woman much like me are underlined. *"Didn't I tell you that if you believe, you would see the glory of God?"*[61]

Time and again He reminds the faltering heart that the way to see glory is to believe. He's got it under control.

---

[60] Lamentations 3:22
[61] John 11:40

The One who governs the sun, guards our coming and going.[62] He who provides seed to the sower will make provision for our every moment.[63] When the baby cries at 2 a.m., when the child slams fingers in the door, when you forget to thaw meat for dinner, when you feel you just can't do it anymore—His mercies are always served fresh and tailor-made.

The difference that marks a life is how one begins her day. Not with stress and strain, not with fear and fret, not with try hard and do better effort, but simple-like, with faith.

*"The great battle of our spiritual lives is, 'Will you believe?' It is not 'Will you try harder?' or 'Can you make yourself worthy?' It is squarely a matter of believing that God will do what only He can do."[64]*

We could live simple like this.

When the day begins and presses down hard, we could resist the urge to take matters into our own hands. We really could live with belief in fresh mercies. We could trust there's manna in our baskets. With the sun before us and the wind behind us and the Glory—the Glory all around us.

---

[62] Psalm 121

[63] 2 Corinthians 9:10

[64] Cymbala, Jim. Kindle Edition: *Fresh Faith: What Happens When Real Faith Ignites God's People,* HarperCollins Publishing, 2011

# ~Day 23~

# Well-Watered

*"It is the Spirit who gives life;
the flesh is no help at all.
The words that I have spoken
to you are spirit and life.
But there are some of you
who do not believe."*
**(John 6:63-64, ESV)**

For weeks, it's been dry around here. The sunflowers are all withered up to a brown crisp and the crepe myrtle's holding her blossoms tight, like unopened gifts. It's just too dry to be giving blessings. The lack of water carries a cost and all of us groan it, waiting for waters to nourish and restore.

Morning comes and I lie in bed, unable to move. Several consecutive nights up with sick children have left me spent. The husband is miles away tending to his own father. And when was the last time I sat down with my Bible for a really good drink?

I'm so thirsty. I don't know how I'm going to make the demands of another day. *Really.* Our bodies are scripted to respond to thirst, parched mouths and weak bodies send signals to our brains that say, "Your survival is at stake! Find water immediately!"

So also our emotional scripts trigger distress signals.

We are programmed with alerts that sound when we are in danger of getting in over our heads. It's the part memory plays. Our limbic system doesn't forget the past. Adoption has taught me that.

My signal is screaming now, telling me I must find relief and fast. *Red alert. Danger. You're going to be over-whelmed and you know you can't handle this. You're on empty and in peril.*

Like many, my script was written in childhood. That's when I experienced a drought so dark and severe it seared a message deep in my memory to avoid similar situations at all costs. When the demands start and the resources are few, the script is replayed and I respond. I bark at the children. I'm short with my husband. I don't give my best. I operate like my reserves are low and back-up isn't coming. It's fight or flight, sheer survival.

I continue to lie there in bed, listening to my scripts. The clock steadily ticks, moving away from 6:02 a.m. and bringing the day on, ready or not. *"You can't do this,"* the messages relay. *"You are too tired. You need rest, a good quiet time, help with the kids, community with others…"* And with each message, I'm pummeled against the pillows, a body of dead weight.

*"Help me, Jesus."* I don't speak the words, hardly even believe them, but they reside deep within and He does too and He responds. *"I will multiply your seed for sowing,"* He reminds me.[65]

---

[65] 2 Corinthians 9:8-11

God gives seed. It is never up to us to create something from nothing. He wants us to take the seed He provides and plant, work, and toil. In faith, He wants us to invest in lives little and big. He wants us to sow seed.

At first, I don't want to listen to the seed talk. It means I must give up my hopes, my desires for rest and reprieve. It means I'll need to reject self-pity, to accept no provision but His grace, and to believe His grace is sufficient. But really, there is no choice but grace. This isn't a fairy tale world I'm living in. But I need to know, is grace really better?

*"You will multiply my seed for sowing,"* I pray back, the first fight of faith. I know this is the moment where a lifestyle is formed. Here is where a woman is made and here is where a single choice makes all the difference of a lifetime.

I swing my legs over the side of the bed and latch on to truth like a dry, hungry infant whose belly needs filling. *Doesn't a baby learn that milk fills, satisfies, nourishes? And can't I take in the Word like milk, find it sufficient to fill all my dry places?*

The clock reads 6:42 a.m. I don't *feel* ready for this. **But faith isn't a feeling. It's a choice.** So I stand on the hardwood floor and I rewrite the script of my life, from "I can't" to "He will."

"He will multiply my seed—He will multiply—He will."

Like dryness, living well-watered can become a lifestyle. It happens one drink at a time, one baby step after another.

One choice at a time, we reject the old script and replace it with the new.

In the kitchen, I glance out the window. I notice it rained during the night. The skies are still gray with moisture. Finally. And the crepe myrtle has opened her gifts. I steal a peek and see hundreds of white blossoms against the dark sky.

*Related Scripture to meditate on today: Psalm 78:19-22*

## ~Day 24~

# Disciple of Grace

**"So after he was raised from the dead,
his disciples remembered that he had said this,
and they believed the scripture
and the saying that Jesus had spoken."
(John 2:22, NET)**

"There's story of an old slave 'round these parts," I begin. Big saucer eyes shine with anticipation and I know *everyone* loves a good story.

"This was back when the Confederacy thought they could up and remove themselves from the Union. But there was one slave owner who decided to free one of his most loved slaves. When the slave owner died, he left his former slave everything he had. It amounted to a little over 50,000 dollars."

Since I'm an accountant, I like numbers. I've looked up what that means in today's dollars. "That's like someone giving you over one *million* dollars," I tell the kids. "So the man was notified of his inheritance and the money was placed in the bank for him. Except months went by and he hadn't withdrawn any money. So the banker went to give him a visit. He explained he had 50,000 dollars available to withdraw. The old slave, who had no understanding of what that meant, asked, 'Well sir, do you think I can have 50 cents to buy a sack of corn meal?'"

I look at my children and they stare back, still waiting for the punch line. Their understanding is no better than that slave's. I explain in the simplest of terms the difference between 50 *cents* and 50,000 *dollars.*

I know it firsthand, how Christians understand the value of money, but not necessarily the incomparable worth of grace. We sing about grace, but then leave church still waiting for the punch line. We know the righteousness of Christ was "credited" to our account. We know that grace means "unmerited favor." We have helpful little acronyms and we talk a whole lot about justification and we can even pitch a celebration service for the $50,000 worth of grace in our spiritual bank. *But are we making daily withdrawals?*

The grace credited to our account wasn't meant to just sit there. Suppose a friend does you straight-up wrong. There's sufficient grace to draw down from, grace in the form of forgiveness. **There are always sufficient funds to give a blessing for a curse.**

And when the children wear and demand and it feels like you just have absolutely nothing left to give, there are sufficient funds credited to your account to give sacrificially, generously, and joyously. We have to believe this! **When the trials blow hard against the soul, there are sufficient funds to stand strong, to persevere, and to get back up.**

This is the grace-oriented life.

Grace was never meant to simply be defined. It was meant to be drawn down upon. And what if we really lived like this? I'm thinking it could be the greatest breakthrough of our lives.

There's story of another slave, one who owed his master. In fact, his debt had accumulated to a sum of millions. There was absolutely no possible way the slave could ever pay the debt, not in several lifetimes.

The slave was called to account and his master told him it was time to pay up. Since he couldn't pay, he and his wife and children would be sold to pay for the debt. The slave begged for mercy. "Just give me a *little more time* and I will pay everything."

In the account, it says the slave asked for a certain type of forgiveness. He asked for "makrothumason," which means an extension of time, a delay.

**Makrothumason requires continual striving, working, performing, and achieving.** This is what the slave assumed he might possibly have a chance at receiving. But the Master was moved with compassion and He granted **full and complete removal** of the debt. He marked the debt *paid in full.*[66]

It was a glorious day, to be granted full pardon! Yet the slave, not realizing he was completely forgiven, thought he still had to collect from others who owed him. He needed every penny he could scrape up to repay his debt. He was still thinking in terms of makrothumason.

He left the meeting with his master, saw someone who owed him a small sum, grabbed him and started choking

---

him to exact payment. And perhaps we fail in our efforts to live the grace-oriented life because we make the same wrong assumption. We believe we can't absorb a wrong-doing. We can't afford to be generous. We can't give a blessing for a curse. We just don't have what it takes. We don't understand grace in terms of full provision, thus we fail to draw down on its inexhaustible supply. As a result, our lives are spent exacting debts from husbands, friends, children, ourselves.

We may have a good theology of grace, but do we live it? Is it in the gut, in the heart, in the reflexes? Is it reflected in our homes, our relationships? Oh God, help us! May it be woven into the fiber of our being, we can trust a full provision sort of grace. At every moment, for whatever need, the bank account is credited beyond our ability to understand and there is no lack.

**"So we keep on praying for you, asking our God to enable you to live a life worthy of his call. May he give you the power to accomplish all the good things your faith prompts you to do. Then the name of our Lord Jesus will be honored because of the way you live, and you will be honored along with him. This is all made possible because of the grace of our God and Lord, Jesus Christ."**

**(2 Thessalonians 1:11-12)**

# ~Day 25~

## The Broken Pitcher

*"Simon Peter answered him,*
*'Lord, to whom shall we go?*
*You have the words of eternal life,*
*and we have believed, and have come to know,*
*that you are the Holy One of God.'"*
**(John 6:68-69, ESV)**

For months it's remained in a box, sitting up there on top of the bookshelf. And when I take it down one night after the kids are in bed, friends stop over and see it lying on the table. They take a look. They even help glue a piece or two on before telling me, "This is a lost cause. Whatever plans you had, you'd best scrap them. Start all over with a new one."

I don't have the heart to tell them that this broken pitcher, shattered into a hundred bits, it represents *me.* One day, when I knew God was breaking me, I needed something tangible to represent what He was doing. So God and I had a ceremony. I went to Michael's and purchased a pitcher. I brought the pitcher home and went out on the patio where I dropped the pitcher on the hard stones. It shattered.

I collected all the pieces and placed them in a box. I wondered how I could ever go back again, how wholeness was possible. But all Christians know that God mends the broken-hearted, right? And even though we can't ever go back to the way things were before the break, we can be healed. *Right?*

So I tried to put the pitcher together again.

*Except I couldn't.* And friends stopped by to help. *They couldn't put it together either.*

I was beginning to resemble Humpty Dumpty. The best advice friends could give was to scrap it and start over again. "It's too shattered," they said. The little ceremony that was to be symbolic turned out all wrong. The pitcher that represented me went into a box and sat in pieces up on the top shelf.

For months and seasons and a year plus of mornings and evenings, it sat.

It gathered dust.

And I wondered what the purpose was? What exactly are we to do with our brokenness?

Until slowly I realized I could stop trying to piece the broken together. A lifetime of trying and effort and striving could never fix me. There isn't a person on the face of earth who can fix me. I began to embrace the broken.

One early dawn, as the pitcher gathered dust on my top shelf, I read of another pitcher that was shattered. This pitcher contained a torch and could this be the lesson I needed to learn—the meaning, the blessedness of brokenness?

"(Gideon) put trumpets and **empty pitchers** into the hands of all of them, **with torches inside the pitchers.** And they blew the trumpets and smashed the pitchers that were in their hands. When they broke the pitchers, they held the torches in their left hands ..." (Judges 7:16, 19-20, NASB)

Doesn't scripture say elsewhere that we are jars of clay—mere pitchers—with the treasure inside?[67] Yet the precious light can only be seen when the jar is broken, when there is nothing left to hide it under,[68] when the shell of self is shattered and broken away.

Brokenness is necessary for the glory that resides within[69] to be seen without.

Which means brokenness is working glory for me.[70] God promises to break but not destroy.[71] Isn't this how Paul came to *boast* in weakness? As he experienced trials, distress, insult, difficulties, and persecution, he moved from *asking* God to remove the hardship to *exulting* in the difficulty. He learned that through these very things the power of Christ dwelt in him.[72] If he learned it, I can, too—we all can. We can learn to embrace brokenness, trusting that it releases the greatness of God.

*What is cracking your pitcher?*

It is true that we grow in dark, silent places and some days the breaking is hard. The seed breaks and births in its dark cave while the world carries on above. There seems to be nothing celebratory about the breaking, about the dying. Yet this is what we have in us, striving to spring forth—Christ in us, the hope of glory!

---

[67] 2 Corinthians 4:7
[68] Matthew 5:15-16
[69] Colossians 1:27
[70] 2 Corinthians 4:17
[71] 2 Corinthians 4:8-9
[72] 2 Corinthians 12:7-10

Through cracked lips, I pray that where there is a broken woman, a shattered momma, others see the glory of God. For when the broken clay pot gets swept into the trash bin, the glory will remain.

The Glory will always remain.

**"Through suffering, our bodies continue to share in the death of Jesus so that the life of Jesus may also be seen in our bodies."**

**(2 Corinthians 4:10, NLT)**

# ~Day 26~

## Martha's Redemption

*"Jesus said to her, 'I am the resurrection and the life. Whoever believes in me, though he die, yet shall he live, and everyone who lives and believes in me shall never die. Do you believe this?'"*
**(John 11:25-26, ESV)**

It's Sunday morning and I'm Martha.

I'm headlong in Sunday dinner preparations while the kids bicker over blankets and which shoes to wear. *How did all those wrinkles wind up on Little Bit's dress?* The angst of it all swells and the cares of this household choke me near to death. Yes, I'm on the way to church and I'm Martha. *How can this be—in the Lord's very presence?* I wonder if I'll ever get it right.

Somehow we arrive at church early. The wind in the trees beckons us outside and we walk the property line with the kids. I stroll under the shade trees, the autumn breeze caressing my skin. Words come, too, brushing up against my angst-filled soul.

*"Now Jesus loved Martha."*[73]

We all know Martha to be the worried, distracted, serving one. But it says it right there in the scriptures that Martha

---

[73] Oh, how I love this simple statement, found in John 11:5!

was loved. My troubled heart leaps. **Jesus loves us Marthas.**

The chronology of the gospels places Jesus' encounter with Martha in John 11—the raising of Lazarus from the dead—*after* His reprimand of her in Luke 10:38. In other words, Jesus did not reprimand Martha, shake His head sadly at her, and then move out of her life. Quite the contrary—He identified her need and arranged a miraculous encounter to resolve it.

While we tend to leave Martha stewing in the kitchen, the Good Shepherd was so tenderized after seeing her distraught and in bondage, He specifically arranged an encounter with her. This special appointment liberated her from her worry-laden, stress-filled service. Isn't that just like our Savior?

Walking the church property, I pace under the trees while the children collect pine cones. My mind races, recalls details from the account in John 11. Jesus loved Martha so much He delayed going to Lazarus. Then Martha met Him on the road to question Him and Jesus wept when He saw her grief. He gave her a powerful "I AM" statement and asked, *"Do you believe this?"*

Surprisingly, the passage regarding Lazarus' death has *Martha's* name all over it. It just might have been her turning point. Before our very eyes we may have the encounter intended to move Martha hearts the world over from angst-filled into hearts that behold the glory of God.

In John 11:40, just before Lazarus is raised, Jesus turns one more time to Martha and says, "Didn't I tell you, if you believe you will see the glory of God?"

"If you believe ..."

What is Jesus saying? *Could it be that Martha's troubled soul could find its rest through trust?* For all her dedication and service, was deep, abiding trust the missing factor in how Martha related with her Lord?

The kids are throwing pine cones across the fence. Someone's hair gets snagged in a branch and she jerks away howling, leaving a few strands dangling, blowing in the breeze. My oldest notices the hanging hair and blurts it out, "Well, God still knows how many strands you have left."

We could trust that.

This same God who counts hair is the same One who says, "Do not worry, just believe." So why all the fretfulness? Isn't fretfulness a failure to simply trust? Stressed like Martha, sinking like Peter, we are overwhelmed by the waves of life. We look away from the One who walks on water, feeds sparrows, and numbers the hairs on our heads. And every time I cave to the swelling tide of noise, hurry, to-do lists, and chaos, it's because I choose not to believe. I choose to believe the noise of turbulence instead of choosing abiding trust in the Savior.

All the while, our Shepherd arranges faith-producing encounters for His followers. He sees the affliction of our souls and walks on water right out to the midst of our turmoil. **"Do not doubt, only believe,"** He gently coaches. He delays the quick fix so that we might truly trust.

To all the Martha's and Matthew's, the Patricia's and Peter's today, Jesus is there asking, "Do you believe this? Do you believe I AM all you need?" And if not, *will* you? Will you trust the One who is All-sufficient?

## Seven "I AM" Statements from the Book of John

Here are some Jesus statements to tuck into your heart. Start believing—in the chaos, in the kitchen, or wherever you might go.

**"I AM the Bread of Life."** Jesus, I will trust You to meet every hunger pang and satisfy every craving of my heart. I will turn to You and I will not be in want.

**"I AM the Light of the World."** Jesus, I trust You to illuminate the darkness and I choose to walk by faith, not by sight. I need not rely on my own understanding.

**"I AM the Door."** Jesus, I trust You to be my security, my safety, and to provide my "good pasture." I will not seek my own grazing grounds, but will trust You to lead me beside still waters.

**"I AM the Good Shepherd."** Jesus, I need not be my own guide or shepherd. Rather, I will listen to and follow Your voice.

**"I AM the Resurrection and Life."** Jesus, I trust You to raise the dead, smelly places within me to new life. I will not rely upon my own self-righteousness or good deeds.

**"I AM the Way, Truth, and Life."** Jesus, I trust You to be the Way when there is none, to speak Truth in a world of noise and turmoil, and to be my very Life.

**"I AM the Vine."** Jesus, I trust You to nourish my soul, to provide the succor and sustenance necessary to produce fruit.

{References: John 6:35, 8:12, 10:9, 10:11, 11:25-26, 14:6, 15:5}

*Note: The third and final time we see Martha in chronology is in John 12. A risen Lazarus is reclining at the table with Jesus, Mary is wiping His feet with her hair, and Martha is serving Him. This trio of worship, three souls redeemed, all brought full circle to life abundant. Jesus didn't leave any of them where they were!*

# ~Day 27~

# Double Blessing

**"Whoever drinks of the water that I will give him will never be thirsty again. The water that I will give him will become in him a spring of water welling up to eternal life."**
**(John 4:14-15, ESV)**

I step over a pile of green mucus the person in front of me hawked on the ground and I board the bus. Body odors and foul air greet me, the stench of the unbrushed and unwashed.

I'm the only fair-skinned one on this bus and I stick out like an alien with purple polka dots.

I'm traveling to a rural town called "Spirit Mountain" and when I arrive, I do sense the spirits, the long-time resident ghosts that have kept this place in darkness.

I take light into the darkness. I proclaim "Yesu" to giddy girls in dorms, to hardened taxi drivers who laugh cynically, to beach-goers who can't get past my white skin and pregnant belly.

Traveling home now, spent. Grimy and smelling myself. Aching back and blistered feet. But I've given my life to Jesus and I'll spend it for Jesus and there is a glory in the work.

Five years later, I'm a virtual hermit, trapped on the sixth floor of an apartment building on the other side of the world with no car, no family, no outlet, not even a back-yard—and four kids, three of them under two years of age and in diapers.

*This is not how I envisioned spending my life for Jesus.*

Even the smells and the spit wads seem more glamorous than *this*.

We love to make trust seem grand. We like big moves of faith. But the Bible talks of walking by faith which means trust isn't so much measured in leaps as it is in steps. Perhaps faith is just this, a cycle of step, fall, catch; step, fall, catch; step, fall, catch. Small steps, baby movements, over and over again.

So I change diapers and make meals and clean snotty faces and wash dirty dishes, and in the midst of it all, I hope for Glory.

That's when I hear it, the story of the thousand-dollar life. Each of us have one, we **are** one. We have been assigned the highest value possible by our Maker. And in our love for our Jesus, we want to lay our lives down on the altar, heave our thousand-dollar bill on the table and live the glorious sacrifice.

God sees our offering and He's pleased. He takes up our thousand-dollar bill, calls us aside, and says, "My precious one, you who I delight over and just can't get enough of, this is what I want from you—*I want you to take your thou-*

*sand-dollar bill to the bank and exchange it for a thousand dollars in quarters."*

How easy to disdain the seemingly trivial choices to trust, to balk at the insignificant sacrifices, those no one sees or cares about. So many mundane choices bear no resemblance of glory. These are the everyday routines that make up the life of a mommy, a father, a preacher no one knows.

We applaud big leaps of faith, large and obvious, yet this is how our Lord wishes to receive our thousand-dollar lives—*in quarters.* Trust steps of small. One meal, one hug, one diaper change, one bedtime story, one day at the office at a time.

Thus the choice of every follower, to willingly hand Him the quarter, do the small, to step-fall-catch, moment after moment. Will we trust we are storing up treasures in Heaven as we slip those coins on the altar? Will we embrace purpose in the mundane through simple trust? Will we invest mere pennies worth of service? **Or will we insist on the "big" work?**

We've given our lives to Jesus and we'll spend it for Jesus and there is glory in the work. Even if it's in quarters. Even if it's in *pennies.* Either way, here's our thousand dollars, sweet Jesus. Sweet Jesus.

# ~Day 28~

## Sacred and Profane

**"Jesus said to her, 'I who speak to you am he.'"**
**(John 4:26, ESV)**

I get her up from her nap. I'm all smiles; she is not. I ask her to go use the bathroom before coming to the kitchen and she does. She goes into the bathroom, stands in front of the toilet, and urinates in her pants.

When I find her there, standing soiled and insolent, I'm immediately irritated.

*I'm sure she's done it to spite me, this child resistant to grace.* "Why did you do that?" I ask her, running on irritation. She stares at me dark, hard, and hostile.

Silence.

I step out of the bathroom, overwhelmed by a sudden sense of my own foundations. I grew up believing God was never pleased and suddenly, I'm aware of the false god I just might be representing to *her*. I pray, "Lord, show me how to parent *this moment* in a manner keeping with Your character."

All my life I reckon I've struggled with understanding God. Perhaps I always will. In this twisted world of jarred chords and evil strains, of figuring out who God really is, I'm learning to let the cross be my middle C.

I leave her in the bathroom to finish washing up while I go outside. I pick toys out of the grass so the lawn can be mowed later without incident. I hear from my Father. *"Do you understand Me now?"* He asks. *"Do you know why I've forgiven, not according to your acts of righteousness? Do you understand it's because of My name's sake?"*

There it is, a beam, and I follow it. Harsh judgment is deserved by us all, but judgment never reflects the entire nature or truest disposition of our God. Words of displeasure, shame, condemnation, and punishment we all deserve for sinning against a Holy God. He can and should dish them out, teach us a lesson we won't forget—except those things don't reflect who He is at His core, a God who is gracious, compassionate, slow to anger, and abounding in loving kindness.[74]

*These things* are His glory.

It is in stark contrast to the punitive version of God I'd always known. For all His right and reason, He desired not to act in a way that our insolent rebellion begged for, but rather in a way that "demonstrated His own love for us."[75] He acted in keeping with His own glorious nature.

*"By this the love of God was manifested in us, that God has sent His only begotten Son into the world **so that we might live through Him**. In this is love, not that we loved God, but that He loved us and sent His Son to be the propitiation for our sins." (1 John 4:9-10)*

In so doing, the true nature and character of God was revealed.

---

[74] Exodus 34:6; When Moses asked God to show him His glory, this is what God revealed.
[75] Romans 5:8

Could this be the root of our search for "the something that's missing"? Could it be that our parenting questions, our consumption of resource after resource, our apathy for the lost, all come back to a deep confusion regarding the true nature of God?[76]

He is good. He is grace. He is love. He invites me to bask in it, believe it, drink it, take it and live. *Live!* And He tells me something else, strong and clear. He tells me to reflect it.

"I've chosen you for this purpose," He says, "And you are to honor Me as I am, as I reveal Myself to you."

The call to trust is always the call to live differently. With each flash of divine revelation into His true nature and character, we are to make lifestyle changes in keeping with His revealed nature. This is what it means to "hallow" His name. The high and noble calling of faith is to sanctify His name, reflect His glory, to be His witness.

I go back inside to a little girl sitting on the toilet. I hug her close. I look deep into her eyes and I stroke damp hair away from her face. I ignore the odor of urine and the wet stickiness against my legs. I smile and offer her my hand.

With a heart full of Glory, I show her God.

---

[76] Bill Bright said, "We can trace all our human problems to our view of God." This bold statement is the basis for the discovergod.com website.

"Then Moses said, 'I pray You, show me Your glory!' And He said, 'I Myself will make *all My goodness* pass before you, and will proclaim the Name of the Lord before you.' Then the Lord passed by in front of him and proclaimed, 'The LORD, the LORD God, compassionate and gracious, slow to anger, and abounding in loving kindness and truth.'"

(Exodus 33:18-19, 34:6)

# ~Day 29~

# Vultures

**"Jesus, knowing that the Father had given all things into his hands, and that he had come from God and was going back to God, rose from supper. He laid aside his outer garments, and taking a towel, tied it around his waist. Then he poured water into a basin and began to wash the disciples' feet and to wipe them with the towel that was wrapped around him."**
**(John 13:3-5, ESV)**

As soon as we receive the text, I begin to fret. Someone has asked Jackson for a favor, a big and costly one, and I know exactly how this is going to go. It's gone this way the whole time we've been married. Jackson is a giver. Close to two decades of marriage has taught me that he'll give and chances are good he'll end up being taken advantage of.

I grumble to him, "Friends stick you with stuff because they know you'll do it. They know good ol' Jackson will literally give the shirt off his back. Why can't someone else be the one to give up the shirt every once in awhile?"

I know it is ugliness boiling up in me. I know it's bitter and corrosive and likely to eat me up. I sound like Job's wife,[77] even to my own ears but somehow I can't stop it.

Jackson looks at me, giving me a wry grin. "Do you know why I do it? I don't do it for them. I do it for God."

---

[77] Job 2:9

I'm glad for him, I really am. I'm glad he can always be the one put out and be fine with it. But I can't. I feel like prey for vultures.

Jackson sees how it eats me, how worried I am about meeting someone else's substantial need while our own needs wait. He gently pulls me aside. "People who trust," he begins and I break down.

Trust. Isn't that what it's always about?

Jackson reminds me that people who trust see the glory of God. "Christians who live closed-handed will never see God in the ways they could have." That's what Jackson tells me and that's how Jackson lives, even if he gets burned.

*God, help me,* I pray as we turn back the sheets on the bed. *I feel so bitter right now and I don't want to be. I want to live open-handedly, even if it does take everything.*

Amidst my brokenness, Jesus speaks. *"Do you remember the widow's mite?"* He asks. *"She gave everything she had. Everything. Do you really think she was the worse off for it?"* His question rouses me, brings laughter to the surface. Of course I don't believe she was worse off, at least that's what I would *say*. But do I *live* that way?

How often do I refuse to give up my last mite, clutching to it tightly like a security blanket? Am I only willing to give out of my excess? Do I profess an all-sufficient Lord but live like He's anything **but** sufficient? And doesn't the test of what I truly believe lie in what I do with my last mite of time, energy, affection, money?

The gentle Savior whispers to me, *"Which would you rather have—your finances shored up, or* trust?*"*

And suddenly, it isn't hard anymore. I'm a blind man seeing again.

There are things more valuable than security and safety. Trust is one of them.

Perhaps it is when we exercise faith to the point of giving that most precious to us that we experience the very nature of God. Yes, I'm desirous of this measure of faith.

**"For God so loved the world that He *gave*..."**

Right there in John 3:16, He offers an invitation. What if, instead of seeing the friend's request as an expense, I trusted God and in that trust, I *gave*? What if I didn't stop at this one need but approached all of life this way? What if, instead of calculating how I could be a minimalist, I became a maximist, seeking to give the absolute most of time, treasure, talent, affection, approval, encouragement, grace, or whatever the moment demanded?

What if, instead of cutting costs, protecting interests, and reserving resources, we got a vision for how we could trustingly *give them up?* By *giving* the last little we have, we could all become maximists. What if this became the mark of our lives?

Lying there in bed, I open the hand and let go. I trust in the God who saw the widow and I give Him my mite. It's this unleashing of the heart, and I discover the essence of the Father.

# ~Day 30~

# Good Girl

***"How can you believe, when you receive glory from one another and do not seek the glory that comes from the only God?"***
**(John 5:44, ESV)**

It's Vacation Bible School and kids swarm thick. Hot bodies race past me in the church hallway, smelling of summer and boys. I breathe deep, remembering a VBS nearly three decades ago, when Ms. Nadine taught our class. We made crosses out of matchsticks.

Dana was in that class, too. Her family had five kids, same as ours. And after a fun day of learning about Christ, Dana's mom walked me out to the car to whisper something in my ear.

"I want my kids to be just like you," she said, admiration glowing in her eyes.

My hungry little heart ate those words. I was starving. Any kind of acceptance is food for an approval-seeking soul. Somehow, I learned it very early in life, that people like good girls. Parents like them, teachers like them, church folk like them, and those were the kinds of folks I hung around.

So I was the good girl. I was the teacher's pet, the "Character Award" winner, the child other parents wanted their kids to be like. But there is one secret a good girl carries deep inside—the stain of sin.  The good girl can't escape the knowledge that she will never **really** be good enough. No matter how much performance, no matter the approval and acceptance she earns, there is still the lusty hunger for more.

And Jesus, He has a way of exposing the lack. He knows how to awaken soul hunger. He knows just how to bring you to the end of yourself. He did it to the crowds in John 6. He led them to a "solitary place" where there was no food, no provision, no resources. There was no goodness. There they remained until their hunger growled and their need hissed and they tasted deep their utter desperation. The Savior's way is always to bring his beloved face to face with their longing and lack, and yes, *especially* their sin. This painful exposure is hard for a good girl.

At the moment the crowd was near faint for lack of provision, Jesus turned to His disciples and said, "*You* give them something to eat."

The disciples not only had nothing for themselves, but now the responsibility to nourish others fell square on their shoulders. How many days have I been in that very spot? I've felt sucked dry, empty? Yet the children are there, the husband, the people I've come here to serve, and Jesus turns and says day after day, "*You* give them something to eat."

The true disciple of Christ comes to the place, again and again, where she lacks, she thirsts, and she has nothing. She has responsibilities but no resources. She longs for adequacy, approval, *goodness*—but there is only want. There is simply all this growling emptiness, us face to face with our inability to ever be enough.

Elyse Fitzpatrick writes of the crowd in John 6, the group of not-enoughs to which we all belong, *"They would have worked, but there was no work to be had that could satisfy such a great need."*[78]

Yes. The good girl, the performer, the fixer. We would do whatever it takes to meet the needs of our heart, of our lives. Heaven knows we try. But the simple truth is, we can't.

Then the Messiah speaks, "Have the people sit down."

Christ makes His intentions clear. He never intended for us to be good enough. He intends for us to sit down, cease our labors, and stop striving and trying while attempting to meet our own needs.

Elyse goes on to say:

> *We too have nothing. We have no innate goodness, no righteousness, no wisdom, no strength, no miraculous power to enable us to work hard enough to meet the overwhelming need of our souls. We are completely bankrupt; we're devoid of the power we need to conquer our sin, to change our nature. We have exhausted all our supplies, and although we are willing to work, there is just nothing that we can do that will satisfy such a wretchedness. We are starving for true righteousness, hungering to be able to meet God's standards, languishing as we try to satisfy the*

---

[78] Fitzpatrick, Elyse, *Comforts From the Cross: Celebrating the Cross One Day at a Time,* Wheaton, Illinois: Crossway, 2009.

*ever-growing needs of those around us. But our Savior calls to us,* "Sit down."[79]

We can hear the call and we can believe it. When faced with our gaping need and unrighteousness, we can sit down and cease striving and trust that He's got us covered. He's handling lunch. He's got our sin taken care of. He's got all of eternity handled. All we need to do is sit down and let Him serve us.

The liberating truth for the not-good-enough is that God never intended us to be good. He intends for us to believe. "For Christ is the end of the law to everyone who believes."[80] And this is the work God has for us, to believe in Him whom He has sent.[81]

We need not be afraid of our hungers, our cravings, our desperation. We need only train ourselves in this, the sitting down and believing. And as we do, there are leftovers. Baskets of abundance.

---

[79] *Ibid.*
[80] Romans 10:4
[81] John 6:29

# ~Day 31~

# The Gift of Weakness

***"Abide in me, and I in you. As the branch cannot bear fruit by itself, unless it abides in the vine, neither can you, unless you abide in me."***
**(John 15:4, ESV)**

It was on the island where she knew. Walking up that mountain path alone, the island breeze gently stroking the skin, she called out to Abba Father and she hears Him whisper, *"Your greatest strength, my child, is that you know you are weak."*

And it is a funny thing, to think that weakness, helplessness, utter need, could ever be anything but a handicap—that it could actually be a gift.

She pondered what Abba said, trekking up that mountain. With so many unknowns, with her baby boy days away from having both eyes cut on, with change looming large, in *sheer weakness,* she treks.

In a world of pretensions, appearances, comparison, and insecurity, a world where she felt small, inadequate, and never enough, she knew it was backwards to really believe weakness is a strength.

But she reads the Word and His words take root and things become simple again.

*"Abiding in Christ is just meant for the weak and so beautifully suited to their feebleness. It is not the doing of some great thing and does not demand that we first lead a holy and devoted life. No, it is simply **weakness entrusting itself to a Mighty One** to be kept, the unfaithful one casting self on One who is altogether trustworthy and true."[82]*

And once again she knows it deep and true. Weakness? Is a gift. She leans hard on the Savior and she abides in His strength, understanding her greatest asset is her own weakness.

---

[82] Murray, Andrew. *Andrew Murray On Prayer*, Kindle Edition: Whitaker House, 2009

# ~Day 32~

# The Hazy City

**"For I have given them the words that you gave me, and they have received them and have come to know in truth that I came from you; and they have believed that you sent me."**
**(John 17:8, ESV)**

The belly of the airbus dips below the clouds and we descend into our new city, home to ten million people. It's known as the Hazy City with its smog and cloud covering. "You'll get used to it," they tell us, referring to the fact that the sun only shines two to three weeks out of the year.

We exit the transport bus after forty-plus hours of no sleep, and Jackson and I promptly get into a fight at baggage claim. I say things I have to apologize for later. I'm thankful the people around me don't understand English. (Rule #1 when traveling: Extra Grace Required when you've been without sleep that long. Rule #2: It's wise to keep mouths shut.)

After three days in a hotel room, our major accomplishments are: purchasing a cell phone, tracking down an outlet adaptor so we can use our computers, and obtaining a bilingual map of the city. The map turns out to be mostly *non*-English. Being illiterate stinks.

The learning curve is steep. It feels like we've twiddled our thumbs for three days and made no progress whatsoever. The cramped quarters of the hotel room only adds to the tension we are all experiencing. We need to locate an apartment, and more immediately, we need to wash clothes. We are down to our last pair of clean underwear and as we all know, that could rapidly become a crisis.

I feel the pull to fret, to focus on the obstacles, to think of everything that is *not* happening. But the Lord brings to mind dinner at Jami's house just a few nights before we left the states and the sign she had hanging in her kitchen which said, **"What are you thinking? Are you thinking of the problem or the solution?"**

Thinking of the problem is natural. Turning the mind towards the solution takes intentionality. It's right before dinner on that third night overseas when Jackson locates the *Daily Light* in the middle of a messy suitcase. He breaks it open right there in the hotel restaurant and reads.

*"You have armed me with strength for battle. When I am weak, then I am strong. Then Asa called to the Lord his God and said, 'Lord, there is no one like You to help the powerless against the mighty. Help us, O Lord our God, **for we rely on You, and in Your name we have come** against this vast army. Jehosaphat cried out, and the Lord helped him."*[83]

The words wash over me, filling me as faith rises within. In His Name we have come to this city. Even though we are powerless, we rely on Him and go out in His Name. God isn't looking for someone who has all the answers or for those who have enough resources to pull the job off. His

---

[83] Scripture compilation from *Daily Light on the Daily Path*, Grand Rapids, Michigan: Zondervan, 1981.

eyes roam to and fro throughout the whole earth in order to strengthen the one who fully trusts in Him.[84]

I am safe as long as I can get my heart to a place of trust.

I find my footing again. Trust is the way of kings and I follow in the steps of Kings Asa, Jehosaphat, and David. More than lineage or ancestry, bowed reliance on God is what makes one *truly noble.* Trust produces royalty; it causes one to rise in warrior strength.

We return to our hotel room, the cramped space with too many suitcases and no A/C. There's no place we call home and we're all wearing dirty underwear. Nevertheless, inside there's this flame of trust in the God who came through for Asa, the God who arms the weak with strength.

As I tuck little ones into double beds and fall weary into one myself, I feel like royalty.

---

[84] 2 Chronicles 16:9

# ~Day 33~

# Magnificent

***"Then he said to Thomas, 'Put your finger here,
and see my hands; and put out your hand,
and place it in my side. Do not disbelieve,
but believe.' Thomas answered him,
'My Lord and my God!'"***
**(John 20:27-28, ESV)**

Her voice is bright and crisp on the line. "Go outside and look on the porch. I just checked and the post office said they delivered you a package this morning."

I don't know what she's talking about. I'd already gone outside that morning and there was certainly no package on the front porch. But I go out again, phone in hand, and there it is, a small white box with USPS tape all over it.

"It's here," I tell her. "What do you want me to do with it?"

My friend says she couldn't bring herself to say goodbye that last evening in Memphis, all of us together, eating pizza on the floor of an emptied-out home. Her eighteen-year-old son said, "I remember we did this same thing the last time you guys left," and we decided right there we'd make it a tradition, pizza on the floor.

On the phone, my friend continues, "I wanted to give you a going away gift, but it was too hard. I was too emotional." She pauses, then adds, "You know I don't do goodbyes very well."

I do know. I know this best friend of mine, this heart sister of fifteen-plus years, I know that *neither of us do good-byes very well.* We've said our goodbyes to one another in Tampa, in Memphis, in Hong Kong, in Richmond. This friend has traveled around the world to enter into my life. Each parting has brought out the ugly-cry, at least on my part. And even though we are hundreds of miles apart now, I know I'm getting ready to have another one.

I start opening the box.

I read the card first which says there's perfume included, "so you can smell good in a very stinky country."

I tease and tell her, "I could be offended at that." We laugh together.

Then I fold the tissue paper away from the small gift. It's a keychain. I hold the smooth surface in the palm of my hand and look at it. My heart leaps. I can't believe what I'm reading. I stand with the phone to my ear, keychain in one palm, and a heart beating so fast I can hardly breathe. There's a stirring within and I know God is here with a surprise present. I'm suddenly aware of each passing second. He is unfolding the moments as a gift and I have a feeling it's *going to blow me to pieces.*

I turn the keychain over, thinking to Him, "I don't know what I'm going to do, Lord, if it says—"

I stop. I can't believe it. I can barely speak. The front of the keychain bears just one word.

**Trust.**[85]

---

"How—um, how exactly did you choose **this** gift?" I squeak out the question, trying to sound normal. I manage to breathe.

"Well, I've been looking for a gift for two months," my friend says. "And for two months, I've had this little keychain sitting on my office desk. But I kept looking and looking. I guess I wanted something more... something magnificent, you know?"

I do know. Who would choose a simple, ordinary keychain as a going away gift, anyway?

And who would choose trust, really? When power seems more magnificent and control, busyness, and a hundred other things seem far more appropriate. But trust? Trust is weak, simple, risky, even silly sometimes.

Yet when we bypass trust, we miss being blown away by God. We miss God-sized surprises because we keep looking for the *magnificent.*

Doesn't the Word say faith rarely seems spectacular? It's just mustard-seed small. Yet as we exercise it, planting that small[86] seed in the soil of our hearts, the tiniest of all becomes a tree of refuge[87] for others.

The tears are dripping down my face onto my shirt. I listen, sensing I'm on holy ground. Only God could have done this, given me a keychain called "Trust" to pull me close and let me feel His heartbeat.

---

[86] Matthew 17:20
[87] Matthew 13:31-32

"So God just kept bringing me back to this little keychain," my friend is saying. "I wanted something bigger and better, but ..."

She trails off and I whisper to her, "It's perfect. It's perfect and I can't even begin to tell you why it's perfect, but it is. This is what God had you give me and it's just perfect."

I sit down at the kitchen table and zip open my Bible. "Listen to this," I tearfully tell her, not even trying to hold back now. "From Deuteronomy 1. I just read it this morning ..."

And I read the sacred words about trust from the page, words written thousands of years ago to the beloved ones of God, words to be taken up by His beloved *today*, regardless of which side of the world you live on.

We share a sister talk about the Word and encourage one another to trust, urged into a belief that steps out into the unknown. "Thank you," I finally tell her. I'm still whispering. Still crying the ugly cry. "Thank you for what you did. Thank you for listening to God and letting Him use you."

And as I say goodbye to a friend I dearly love and miss, I tuck a keychain into my pocket. With it, a reminder to trust God, to plant that small seed, to stop looking for the magnificent and instead unwrap each moment in awestruck trust. For she who believes in Him will never be disappointed.

## Five Things You Can Trust God for as You Step out into Today

{Deuteronomy 1}

Today, the Lord goes before you. Moment by moment He leads the way. You can trust that.

Today, the Lord will fight for you, just as He always has. You can count on that.

Today, the Lord will carry you ... like a father carries his son. It's a guarantee.

Today, the Lord will search out resting places for you. He knows you are but dust. You can trust Him.

Today, the Lord will show you the way to go. He will not keep His will hidden. He will make known to you the path of life. You can step out on solid footing.

## ~Day 34~

# Family Values

**"When they got out on land, they saw a charcoal fire in place, with fish laid out on it, and bread. Jesus said to them, 'Come and have breakfast.'"**
**(John 21:9, 12, ESV)**

It all started when I asked her to pick up. Company is coming and an entire evening is planned. I really don't have time to work through some issue that no one really understands in the first place.

When she goes rigid, refuses to answer questions, just sits there sour upon being asked to pick up, I want to give up. Throw in the towel. I'm sick to death of the whole mess. Wounded children and exasperated mommas and adoption and being like Jesus—it's all just one big pulsing heartache.

No, I'm not going to walk out on anybody. I'll smile at the guests and talk about how great God is. I'll be a decent mom and wife. But there's more than one way to be a quitter.

Inside is where the quittin' starts. There's the quiet, insidious choice to just stop believing.

Here's the thing: when we stop believing God, we start believing something else. And on day 1,897 of the battle, I just want to call it quits, stop believing for something greater. Inside, I want to stop trying. Stop acting like anything is ever going to change.  Stop pretending there is something glorious about it all. Truth is, there's nothing glorious about the wretched mess.

Truth is, sometimes it's just too much to believe for anything better. It's too hard to *keep* believing when everything tells you to *get real already*. When day after day you go at it like a bull rider, out to master the beast, holding on with every tenacious strand of your being. Every day you're thrown in the mud while your confidence—your hope—gets slung and trampled. Well, there's only so long you can keep doing that.

The vision can be smeared by the mud. The laying face down in muck can rob you sheer blind. Your faith can be eroded by the maddening mundane.

I sit there on her window seat, defeated. We talk the same talk as always. They are just words now. My heart's not in it. I speak Truth, but it's hollow. I hear company at the door. She starts bawling and sniffling and one really can wonder how in the world a mom is supposed to do this jig. Day after lousy day.

And then it comes to me: our family crest.

We agonized for a year or more over which four family traits we wanted to capitalize on. Which four values did we want etched into stone; which ones would make the cut and go on the family crest?

One of the four we decided on was diligence.

And how many times have I told the kids when they wanted to quit at something too hard for them, "Remember our family value? Part of being diligent means we keep going. We keep trying. We don't ever give up."

Never give up.

It strikes me then. It's a Family Value,[88] straight from the Father Himself. It's a highly prized character trait and all God's children are instructed in it.

He taught us to pray and never give up, to know that the testing of our faith works patience, to persevere through trials and not let go of our confidence. Our Daddy told us that no matter what, we must build ourselves up in our "most holy faith."[89]

**Never give up.**

And I hear the Father instructing this child's heart, "You can't quit, my girl. Because perseverance is a family value and you're in the family."

And through my gritted teeth I say it out loud before my mind has time to negotiate, "I'm not giving up. I am *not* giving up."

The tears are coming down her face and now they're coming down mine, too—the blood streaks of battle. There's company waiting to be greeted, but I've got unfinished business to take care of.

"I'm not giving up!" I say it loud, blazing a trail of faith. I'm pacing the room, waving fists in the air, and I'm doing warfare that can't wait, the inner battle in unseen places where souls are negotiated for.

Don't the scriptures show that the course of an entire family can be traced back to the map of one person's

---

[88] Luke 18:1-8
[89] Jude 21

unwavering faith? I lay down my legacy. "Do you hear me?" I say it strong, more confident now:

> *When the Son of Man comes, He's gonna find persistent faith in this corner of the earth! I am not giving up! I've got the promise of my righteous Daddy to defend and protect and avenge me speedily. He's able to keep what I've entrusted to Him. He's going to take this sorry mess and He's going to do abundantly above and beyond all I ask or think. He is going to keep us from stumbling and make us stand faultless before His glorious throne with great joy one day. Boy, howdy, I'm not givin' up.*

And in the midst of my faltering heart, I know it sure, a wounded child doesn't need her momma to be perfect. She just needs her to be persistent. Persistent in faith.

A faltering daughter doesn't need her momma to have all the answers. She just needs her to have all faith. A wayward child doesn't need her parent to keep pining over regrets. She just needs her to keep beseeching the Father. And a teen finding his way doesn't need a momma who frets and controls, he just needs a momma who, in confidence, takes it all to the throne time and again.

**The world needs mommas who won't quit believing. Who never give up.**

And just for today, I am one.

"I tell you, as for God, He will defend and protect and avenge them speedily. However, when the Son of Man comes, will He find persistence in faith on the earth?"

(Luke 18:8)

## ~Day 35~

# Subway Salvation

*"When Jesus had received the sour wine,*
*he said, 'It is finished,' and he bowed*
*his head and gave up his spirit."*
**(John 20:31, ESV)**

It's raining when I leave. I say an early morning goodbye to the kids and the hubs to attend my first day of University. *For the second time.* Me, pushing forty.

The subway is crowded and my pant legs are muddy. I stand scrunched in a corner next to a man who uses my head as a prop for his morning newspaper.

Somewhere near the Dongmen Bridge it happens. A man standing in car #105513 passes out. I see the crowd move like a tidal wave away from him. Bodies circle around where he lays collapsed. From my corner spot, I see his legs protruding from the circle of bystanders.

Everyone seems frozen. Are they unsure? Or uncaring? I wonder if the man is traveling alone. Is there anyone here who can help him?

No one steps forward. No one stretches out a hand.

Just as suddenly as his collapse, the man scrambles to his feet and white-knuckle grips the overhead handle bar. A few standing close start to snicker, undoubtedly relieved the ordeal is over. Someone has the sense to give up their seat. He stumbles to sit, sinks back and leans his head against the side of the car.

He's sitting on the same side I'm on, about 15 feet away and I watch him. He's young, maybe 25? Then he groans and closes his eyes. We are all riveted.

When he starts to slide down on top of the gal beside him, I know he's passed out again. She reaches out and tries to push him off but she can't. She's holding him up, looking wild at the passengers around her. She's panicked and desperate. Her eyes plead for someone to help.

Not a soul budges. Everyone stands and stares, not moving a muscle.

The man needs medical attention. Why doesn't someone near him make a phone call? Push the emergency button? Yell for medical assistance? *Something?* I'm just a foreigner, an outsider. I'm no one's savior.

But I can't wait any longer. I hoist my bag and push my way through 15 feet of people. I grab him with both hands and gently right his unconscious body. "This man needs medical attention. Where is the emergency button on this subway?" I ask.

No one knows. Everyone seems relieved that someone has stepped forward. *Like I know what I'm doing.* I don't. I ask a woman nearby to contact the subway's security. "I don't know how to call them," she tells me.

Why won't somebody **do** something?

The man is still out and he's lost control of his bladder. Urine drips down the seat, puddles the floor. Another stop comes and goes and we're still trying to get help.

The young man briefly comes to and tries to sit up. "It's okay," I tell him. My hands are on his shoulders. He blacks out again. "Where is that emergency button?" I keep asking. I finally find the button and press it.

Nothing happens.

I've been elected in charge so I'm making the executive decision. "When we stop, someone needs to get off and alert security that this passenger needs medical attention," I tell the passengers. I'm staying with him. At the next stop, a woman jumps off and starts yelling for security. The train shuts the doors and leaves without her...and without help.

The young man's face is beaded with sweat. He opens his eyes and looks at me. There is green matter rolled in the corner of his left eye. "We're going to help you," I reassure him. My hands still hold him tight. I'm straddling urine.

His body relaxes. "Thank you," he whispers.

Security is standing on the platform at the next stop. We are able to get the young man off the subway and to the medical station. I see him to safety and continue on to my stop. It's still raining when I exit the subway station, the world above oblivious to the cares of single soul struggling in the bowels below. I dodge puddles and oncoming traffic as I walk to the university. I can't help but wonder, *"What if it had been me on that subway? Would anyone have come to my aid?"*

I'm pretty sure of the answer.

And there comes a time in a person's life when she senses her own deep helplessness, her raw need, her vulnerability, her sheer isolation. Past our exteriors and our busyness, our smiles, successes, or accomplishments, deep in the bowels of the soul, we know we're depraved deep and broken to boot. And no one is capable of reaching us. No one can bridge the gap. No one can put us back together.

I groan guttural with David, *"Look to the right and see: there is none who takes notice of me; no refuge remains to me; **no one cares for my soul"** (Psalm 142:4, ESV).

Surely we all are that young man on the subway. But there's something else. There's another whisper flooding in, giving hope, speaking truth. God's voice speaks as One who takes notice of man.

**"I looked, but there was no one to help; I was appalled, but there was no one to uphold. So my own arm brought me salvation, and my wrath upheld me."**
**(Isaiah 63:5, ESV)**

And it's the Good News we can cling to, that when there was no one to step in and rescue, God Himself donned flesh and came down to dwell among men. God ate with sinners[90] and He spit in dirt[91] and He asked, "Do you believe?" And He said to the broken, "Your sins are forgiven."[92]

The profane is transformed by the Sacred, the broken redeemed by a Lamb, the dead given new life.

We have a Savior.

It's just that in the midst of the mud and the mess and the mundane, we need reminders. On that muddy walk to the university, I notice the bottom of my bag smells of urine.

Once inside the University, I duck into the bathroom to wash my hands. Glancing in the mirror, I'm surprised to see the cross prominently hanging around my neck. I had forgotten I was wearing it. The gold shines beautiful there against the black backdrop of my top.

The cross. God's message to us, His assurance that everything really is okay. The cross! I pray the young man and train passengers saw the cross today, dangling from the neck of someone who said, "I'll help you."

The cross speaks truth when we're desperate lost and need to know there's a way.

The cross says when we were without hope in this world—Jesus came.

When we were aliens and strangers—Jesus came.

---

[90] Mark 2:13-17
[91] John 9:6
[92] John 8:11, Matthew 9:1-7

When we were separated, isolated, excluded from citizenship—Jesus came.

When we were **dead** in our transgressions and sins—Jesus came.

He hoisted the cross and He bridged the gap. He went the distance and reached out to rescue the needy. With complete competency and wild devotion, He said, **"I will help you."**

There in the mirror, I look at the cross against the backdrop of black. In my weakness and inability and failure, smelling of urine and mud, I hear its message afresh: **"Don't be afraid, you little Jacob. I will help you."**[93]

It's the hope of the redeemed that changes her life. It's the truth that propels her onto the streets, into the classroom, onto the subways.

The cross changes everything.

We're redeemed.

---

[93] Isaiah 41:14

# ~Day 36~

# Clothed

**"He who saw it has borne witness—**
**his testimony is true, and he knows that he**
**is telling the truth—that you also may believe."**
**(John 20:35, ESV)**

The birds are my quiet time this morning.

There is no tranquil lake setting, no leisure morning with coffee. No quiet pre-dawn meditation. Just the high-rise lifestyle of living and working in a city of ten million people.

I get up 15 minutes before kids, chaos, and the breakfast rush. Before the dressing and the brushing, before the backpacks and the inevitable shoe search.

It's not the way I prefer to do it, but some days, just getting out of bed is an accomplishment.

After I get the kids to school, I walk half an hour to the bus stop. It's *my* turn to go to school and today, I've got a presentation to make. My laptop weighs heavy on my back. Anxiety pounds the pavement with each step as the prospect of presenting a controversial topic in a foreign language among classmates half my age weakens my knees and slows my steps. A soul can grow right weary. Where is backbone when you need it?

Around me cars speed, horns honk, and buildings rise. Someone correctly said that whenever you don't have time for God is when you need Him the most. I pray. I need vision. Faith. Solid footing. I need boldness to speak the Name. I need fresh Glory to fill me.

Overhead, a flock of black birds takes flight. He speaks. *"Consider the birds of the air. They worry not. Neither should you."*

The dawn comes with that. Its light shines pure grace.

Those winged creatures woke early with no idea where or how they were going to find food. *They weren't worried.* They sang. In utter trust and reliance upon their Maker, they took to the skies.

I could, too.

**"Consider the flowers of the field. I clothe them with beauty and grace. I'll clothe you, too."**[94]

And with that, my quiet time happens walking down that sidewalk in a city of ten million people.

We can accessorize with Prada and perfume, we can don titles and accept flattering labels, and we can forget the simple beauty of grace. When faced with our lack and weakness, we can forget the birds and forget the blossom was once a mere seed—but God clothed it.

He does that. He clothes and gives a bare body glory.[95] I board the bus and arrive at school. When it's my turn, I

---

[94] Matthew 6:25-34

speak the Name. I'm counting on those clothes of glory—
no Prada or silk here.

The teacher texts me after class. "I'm so happy you are in
my class," she says. "I'm a Christian, too." And I can't
believe what I'm reading! I ask Jackson to read the message to verify I really am translating it correctly.

Yep, Teacher Gui is a Christian.

I have no idea how this will all unfold. I don't know what
God is up to. But I'm pretty sure it's abundantly above and
beyond what I could ask or think.

The next day, Teacher Gui asks me to stay behind after
class. We talk in hushed tones about the Savior, about
Sunday worship and the Bible. She tells me again how
happy she is I'm in her class. Her happiness has nothing
on mine.

Something impossible grows, sprouts from the small, the
raw.

> It's wonderful to think of the fact that God can turn
> around a whole nation, a whole world, by using
> us. God uses simple things, you know that. He us-
> es simple, mundane, everyday, routine, common
> things for the most amazing purposes. When He
> made man in the Garden, **He didn't use gold, sil-
> ver, or even iron; He used dirt.** That ought to
> give you an idea of how He works right from the
> start. When He called David to deliver Israel from
> the Philistines, He didn't want Saul, the great king,

*and He didn't want Saul's massive armor. He used a shepherd and a couple of stones, that's all. When He came into the world, He didn't enter the family of the wealthy and noble, He didn't find Himself born in a castle;* **He simply chose a peasant girl and a stable.** *When He chose the Twelve, He didn't choose the elite, educated, and affluent. He just chose a group of* **ignorant Galileans.** *The Bible says,* **'Not many mighty, and not many noble.'** *That's the way it always has been, because God gets the greater glory in the humbleness of the one that He uses. So He uses us, grains of sand, to influence a corrupting world.*[96]

When did I start expecting to outgrow child-like reliance? At what age did I think I'd lose the desperation? When did I expect to be mighty and noble? Prestigious? Competent?

God uses the weak, the base, the foolish.

And praise God, I still qualify.

---

[96] MacArthur, John. In sermon entitled "You Are the Light of the World." www.gty.org. Accessed September 7, 2014, <www.gty.org/resources/sermons/2208/you-are-the-light-of-the-world>

# ~Day 37~

## Pineapples and Pride

*"Truly, truly, I say to you, unless a grain of wheat falls into the earth and dies, it remains alone; but if it dies, it bears much fruit."*
**(John 12:24, ESV)**

She stands in front of the toy bin, both arms around an overflowing red tub of tinker toys and box cars. She tries to slide the tub into the bin slots, but the tub is too big to fit. She's going to need help. But I know my Little Bit. She doesn't like admitting her need for others. I can see it on her face, the pride pressing her to go it alone, to avoid being vulnerable, to be independent instead.

I offer her a path out of her predicament, the way of escape before she digs herself into an unsavory situation. "Little Bit, do you think that tub is going to fit?"

"No," she replies, a tinge of whine to her voice.

"What do you think you should do?" I prompt her, offering a magic feather. It helped Dumbo fly and I want my girl to soar. All she has to do is ask for help. But she doesn't take the way offered, doesn't want the help.

She decides to go it alone. "I need to get a stool," she tells me.

Even with a stool, she can't reach the top slot. She knows just as much as I do that sliding the tub into the top bin is a flat-out impossibility. But there she is, looking a fool while trying to balance on her tiptoes on a stool top. Her arms are filled and aching, her back arching. Listening to the voice of pride always puts one in a precarious, foolish position.

"Little Bit," I try again. "Do you think you can slide that tub in?"

"No," she says, still hard and independent.

"Well, what do you think you should do?"

She starts crying. Admitting her dependence, her need, is just about to kill her. Asking for help seems unbearable. It is painful. It is threatening. **That's how it is when you've been lied to**. When you've depended on somebody and they left you in a cardboard box on the day you were born. When you needed someone to care for you and they took the liberty to take a cigarette lighter to your genitals, darkness is there. But it isn't the darkness that damages so much as it is the lies that accompany. *Can we just get that already?*

You can leave behind cardboard boxes and cigarette lighters. You can leave behind past identities and bad choices, and the good news is that you really can be rescued out of darkness.

It's the lies that we aren't so quick to let go of. They move in. They tell us we're better off alone. "You can't trust anyone," the serpent whispers. *"You're safer this way."* And we believe and we act on our beliefs. We establish an entire way of life around a lie.

"What do you think you should do?" I ask her again. Crying, Little Bit finally asks for help. I reach out and take the tub from her. We finish picking up and, afterwards, we talk about pride. I sit on the stool with her in my lap. "Pride is not your friend," I tell her. "Pride will isolate you and steal from you. When you hear pride telling you not to ask for help, don't listen to it. Tell it 'no!' It is not your friend!"

"It's okay to ask for help. Jesus tells us to ask and we'll receive," I say as I wipe away her tears.[97] She shudders relief in my arms.

After lunch, we all go for a walk. Hawkers and street vendors are out selling their goods and we buy fresh sugar cane sticks for the kids. Jackson spots peeled, whole pineapples and we approach the vendor to ask how much.

He eyeballs us and says, "Eight dollars."[98]

I'm put off. No doubt the man is giving us the jacked-up foreigner price.

"That's ridiculous," I tell Jackson. "Let's go."

I burn my bridge. As we meander, we finally stop in a small grocery store for some bananas. Jackson picks out a pineapple to boot. When we get to the cash register, the pineapple price rings up $23.60.

I gulp. And fork out the money. Three times the money we would have paid the street vendor.

---

[97] Matthew 7:7 and Matthew 21:22
[98] In local currency, about $1.30 USD

When we get outside I call Little Bit. "Little Bit, Momma just listened to her pride."

"You did?" She looks up at me, face beaming. She is excited to hear it. I laugh.

"Yes. I did." I tell her about how I rushed off from the vendor without asking for a discount, without giving him any further ado. I snubbed the man because he gave me the slightest injustice.

"That was pride talking and I listened. Because of it, I ended up paying three times more for my pineapple."

By this time all the kids had huddled around me on the sidewalk in front of the grocery and were listening to my story. **"Did you cry?"** Little Bit asks.

The question seems peculiar. Yet I remember it comes from one who has known the isolation and pain of pride firsthand. How many times has her pride held her back from joining in, from engaging, from being vulnerable, from attaching, *from belonging?*

Oh my, I do believe she has just realized pride hurts.

"I did not cry," I tell her, "but my heart hurts in here." I tap my chest and inwardly I go low before God. *"Oh Jesus, forgive me!"*

Little Bit takes my hand. We begin to walk again. The other kids skip ahead, chewing sugar cane. Little Bit and I lag behind. She looks up at me. "Momma, I love you."

God does give grace to the humble. There's the grace of daughters and the grace of forgiveness and there's grace to renounce the lies and the self-sufficiency. There's grace to trust. I look down into my Little Bit's upturned face and smile. Right there on a dirty sidewalk at the backside of nowhere, two girls broken by pride are joined by humility. We squeeze hands and smile and walk on.

Together.

# ~Day 38~

# Small Things

**"Early in the morning he came again to the
temple. All the people came to him,
and he sat down and taught them."
(John 8:2, ESV)**

I wanted to reflect something amazing.

I wanted to live something noble.

I wanted the Divine to invade in such a way that we all stood in awe of His glory.

But then the kids got up whining.

They fought through breakfast and one wiped his snotty nose on the couch and we stumbled out the door late and I had to take Little Bit to the doctor.

It was rush hour as we literally squished ourselves onto a subway that was packed like sardines with people who had bad breath and B.O.

Once we arrived at the hospital to have blood drawn, we entered this open-air hall crowded with nearly a thousand people—**all of them there to have blood drawn.**

It was hot and stuffy and there were no chairs and the wait was long. That ache for glory, for something noble and worthy, it seemed to slip away, further and further beyond reach.

I could feel the slipping, the slow death, the faith and hope being wrung right out of me by a thief I couldn't even see.

And I wondered what a person is to do when life has starved her of what really matters. How does she regain faith when it's been lost? How does a hope-deprived heart regain its health? How does a perishing woman apprehend her lifeline, that glimpse of Glory, before it's too late?

I'm standing in that huge outdoor hall, waiting our turn for the needle, when the woman beside me asks about my Little Bit. "Her parents didn't want her?" she asks. **"Was she abandoned?"**

I wince at such a cruel question, like I'd been elbowed in the gut. Because I *am* her mother. *We are* her parents. But it was asked in ignorance, so I overlook the words and speak to the heart of this woman. "My Little Bit was left in a cardboard box the day she was born. But we are her family now."

We chat a few minutes more. **I want it to be enough.** I want to go back to just waiting, go back to being numb. I want to retreat into my shell of no-risk living. Hoping for Glory is just too painful. It makes the heart ache.

And yet. I know this is an opportunity for me to share the good news of Jesus. On the one hand, I want to hope for Glory. I want to live the Christ-life. On the other, I just feel so tired. I've done this so many times before; it all seems canned, mechanical—so futile. But there's the prompting inside, that internal force, the tidal wave of hope, as if He's laid His hand on me and I cannot help but speak up.

So I do.

I can't say that my heart is totally in it. I'm not full of faith that something miraculous will happen as I open my mouth. I just, simply, **begin.**

"I'm a Christian," I tell her. "We adopted because adoption is what God does for us. He brings us who are without hope into His family."

And no sooner do the words leave my mouth than the lady beside me flails her arms and reaches for her purse. She's a crazy woman, digging deep in the bowels of her bag. She comes up with a pack of tissues just in time. She bursts into tears.

"I'm a Christian, too," she sputters, dabbing madly at her eyes. "Just haven't been to church in a very long time."

I'm shocked. You don't meet Christians like this here. Not in this country—not in a hot, crowded, smelly hallway where you are just one anonymous person. I voice a few more words, awkward and tentative. I don't know where to go with this. I'm listening for His prompting to direct my words, guide my speech.

The life of Christ fills me then and I *do* know. I know why we're here, why years ago we left father and mother on the other side of the world. I know why we squeezed into a subway that morning and stood lost in a crowd of a thousand. I know. It's so we could stand next to this one woman and be the Father's voice—*her Father's voice*—to her. "You are very special," I tell her. And **I'm really just relaying a message from our Daddy.**

"There is something He wants you to do, some way you can serve, and no one else can do it. He's prepared you for it and He's given you this ministry. You are tailor-made for this job."

Tears are dripping down her cheeks and her heart is soaking up words that are not mine. We are two crazy ladies crying in public. Everyone around us stares and I've a mind to let them in on the joyous secret:

**God draws lambs into His fold.** He restores hope to His people.

We all like big shindigs. We want church planting movements, big followings, best sellers, and we don't want to settle for anything less than A.W.E.S.O.M.E. I get that.

But God whispers to our child-like hearts, "Don't ever despise the day of small things."[99]

The Lord **rejoices** in the small beginnings. He is, after all, the God who leaves the 99 for the **one.**

And sometimes you can know it at the strangest of times, like in the midst of a very ordinary day when your kid smears snot on the sofa and you feel your inadequacies and you stand next to someone with body odor. You can

---

[99] Zechariah 4:10

know that in spite of *everything that's wrong with you,* God has given you the ministry of reconciliation. You can know He's made you alive in Christ.

> *I come as one who desires, who seeks, to be prepared to live out the life of Christ today on earth, to translate His hidden heavenly glory into the language of daily life, with its dispositions and His duties.*
>
> *As I think of all my failures in fulfilling God's will, as I look forward to all the temptations and dangers that await me, as I feel my entire insufficiency and yet say to God, "I come to claim the life hid in Christ, that I may live the life for Christ." I feel urged and drawn not to be content without the quiet assurance that God will go with me and bless me.*
>
> *May I indeed expect to live the life hid with Christ in God, so as to make it manifest in my mortal body? I may. For it is God Himself will work it in me by the Holy Spirit dwelling in me. The same God who raised Christ from the dead, and then set Him at His right hand, has raised me with Him and given me the Spirit of the glory of His Son in my heart. Believe what God says about you. Accept what God has bestowed upon you in Christ. Take time before God to know it and say it. The life of every day depends on it."* [100]

---

[100] Murray, Andrew. *The Master's Indwelling*, Public Domain

*TRUST without BORDERS*

# ~Day 39~

# Light in the Darkness

**"The true light, which gives light to everyone, was coming into the world."**
**(John 1:9, ESV)**

In her book, *Lessons I Learned in the Dark,* Jennifer Rothschild tells the story of how she slowly lost her eyesight. At the age of 15, she was legally blind and doctors told her there was no cure for her condition... and no hope of ever regaining her sight.

Jennifer says,

> *I know well the trappings of blindness. I understand the isolation and hardships it can bring. Yes, blindness can be painful—all life's heartaches are—but through it, God has taught me the greatest lesson to be learned in the school of suffering: Even when it is not well with our circumstances, it can be well with our souls. This is the first and greatest lesson I learned in the dark, and the foundation for all the lessons that have followed.*[101]

Perhaps you know well the trappings of unbelief. You understand the darkness of doubt and the fear of distrust. While unbelief may be a temptation, it need not be what defines us any longer. Hebrews 11:1 says, "Now faith is

---

[101] Rothschild, Jennifer. *Lessons I Learned in the Dark*, Colorado Springs, Colorado: Multnomah Books, 2002.

being sure of what we hope for, being convinced of what we do not see" (NET).

Faith means that we place our trust in *something we can't see.* Jennifer Rothschild explains it like this, *"If we understand this is what faith is, we can exercise it in the confidence the apostle Paul talked about when he said we walk by faith, not by sight.*[102] *Walking by faith is acting upon a reality not yet seen."*

Perhaps you are like me, you've lived most of your life according to what you can see or what you can feel. The call to trust is a call to act according to what we can't see but believe to be true because God said so. It's a choice.

Isn't it time, my friend? Time for your soul to be settled even when your circumstances are not? Isn't it time to see with spiritual eyes? It takes practice, sure. But what better way is there to live?

Here is a final exercise I've found helpful in choosing trust.

## Developing Your Night Vision

- **Sit down and list all the attributes of God** you can think of. Slip these attributes on as your night goggles.

- **Take your dark circumstance and view it through God's attributes.**

---

[102] 2 Corinthians 5:7

Example: "Because God is both kind and wise, He arranged these (fill in the blank) circumstances in my life." Ask Him to show you His goodness, nature, wisdom, and kind purposes in *this* and to help your unbelief. Repeat this when fears, doubt, and distrust creep back in.

- **Turn promises into weapons.** Romans 4:20-21 says that Abraham battled unbelief by reminding himself of the promise of God. If we neglect the promises of God, we are only half-prepared for battle. It is through recalling specific promises that we resist the temptation to doubt and unbelief. If you haven't already, take a few moments to list out the specific things you doubt God on. Then find promises in scripture regarding these areas and write them out. Review these promises as you are tempted to unbelief.

**You can watch a five-minute video presentation of Jennifer here:**

**http://www.youtube.com/watch?v=dzcpIP0JI6k**

# ~Day 40~

# Jesus

**"Now Jesus did many other signs in the presence of the disciples, which are not written in this book; but these are written so that you may believe that Jesus is the Christ, the Son of God, and that by believing you may have life in his name."**
**(John 20:31-31, ESV)**

The bus swerves on the mountain road and I look straight down from my window seat to see sheer drop. Nothing but mist lies beneath us. We are mere centimeters from death. Mountain climbers call this *exposure*, the condition of "being on high vertical rock with full consciousness that nothing exists between you and the distant ground but thin air."

And there are times in one's life when you come into full consciousness, when you know nothing exists between you and death but the invisible sustaining of God. My visit to the orphanage was one of those times.

The orphanage juts from the side of the mountain and as we climb the steps to enter, I see faces of children peeking out from behind doors. We enter and spread food out on tables. Children run up to snake packages of cookies, crackers, and candy into their pockets. Some sit down to eat the fried chicken we brought; others just hoard, waiting for their own private feast.

All the children but one have special needs. The healthy children get adopted out to homes around the world. The rest stay behind.

"If you have any language ability," the director of the trip tells us, "please spend time talking with the children."

That's me. I've worked hard to learn this difficult language. The thought crosses my mind: *What if I've learned this language for a time such as this? Just for today, to communicate the love of Christ to children abandoned up the side of some mountain in the middle of nowhere?*

So I approach child after child, see mouths of rotten teeth and clothes with holes in them. I offer warm arms and warm words and I pray Christ takes broken pieces and mangled words and nourishes the hungry soul anyway.

Then, I'm standing by the director of the trip when she says to the group, "There is one child that hasn't come out. The child is tied up in the room next door." A child tied up? Mercy. My heart starts to pound.

"They told me the child can come out if someone takes the child and does not leave their side." The director says this and I see raw panic in the eyes of our group. So does the director. We all want to run from what we can't predict, what we can't make sense of, avoid what is risky and unknown.

The director turns to me. "Arabah, will you take this child?" I stammer, "Yes, of course," and follow the house-parent to the room where the child is tied.

It's a girl standing at the window.

Her hair is chopped short and it's hard to tell if she's a girl or boy with her clothing, but I look in her face and I see the spirit of a girl, the feminine beauty mirrored in my own heart. I want to cry. The window is open, even in this cold, and she is tied to a security bar at the window. Her eyes are bright as I take her hands into mine. Her skin is freezing.

I look in her eyes and speak softly, asking if she wants to go outside for awhile. The rule is that I must keep her on the "leash," a thick strip of fabric tied around her torso, and that no matter what, I can't feed her.

I soon find out why. She rushes the food tables and grabs trash off the floor to eat it. She knocks snacks out of other children's hands while stuffing food and debris down her throat. I adjust to this child. A child with food issues. I smile inside, thinking of my Little Bit. I can do this.

I steer her away from the food tables, but not before grabbing a wrapped bun. The house parent told me not to give her any food, that this little girl who lives tied up had already eaten.

I don't listen. I give her the wrapped bun. She tries to eat it, only to realize it is secured by packaging that she can't open.

"Wo bang ni," I tell her. "Let me help you."

I want her to receive food from a stranger, to know generosity, to realize there is kindness. After a life of abandonment and abuse, pain and isolation, I want to move her one step closer to trust. She needs to know there is hope, there is a good future. There is a Maker who is also a Father. *Is this not why we go in His name?*

It seems preposterous for me to try to communicate to her that she doesn't have to self-protect and look out for her own interests. Me of all people, and she who has lived in a dog-eat-dog world. This is a stretch for sure that seems better left undone. But I try anyway. I get down on her level, face to face, and repeat the words to her again and again, "I can help you. I will open it for you. You are so special and so beautiful. Slow down, everything is okay."

She glances up at me quickly. Amidst the rush around us, somehow that inner need for survival is momentarily overpowered by trust. She looks at me and **hands me the bun.**

I rejoice at the victory. I open the package and give her the bread. She devours it.

We repeat this over and over until she's had chicken, buns, cookies, crackers, juice.

I spend an hour with my little friend, oblivious to everything else going on. At the end, she finds a shiny gold ornament that fell off the Christmas tree. She picks it up and for the first time, she smiles. She speaks, holding the ornament, rolling it around in her cold hands.

"It's yours," I tell her. "You can have it." I speak words of love over her. When it is time to go, I ask the house-parent to take her. "No," she tells me, "You must go tie her back up."

It's one of the hardest things I've ever done in my life...tying a child up.

And then leaving.

But as I get ready to leave the room, I notice I'm the only adult there and many of the other children have returned. They are lined up in wheelchairs and every single one of them is staring at me, with hopeless eyes. I touch each one and try to speak words they can understand.

They don't. Their eyes tell me the words are meaningless. They stare at me dark, hopeless, and empty. So I speak just one word, *The Word,* again and again and again. It's the only one they need know, really.

**Jesus.**

"Don't forget," I tell them. "Jesus, Jesus, Jesus."

It seems such a pitiful attempt in the face of such pain and hopelessness. When the dark emptiness stretches endlessly before them. It seems so meaningless, so impractical. Why bother? Why pretend that it matters, that it is somehow significant?

When I return home, I cry with Jackson as he tells me there are more headlines of death and loss and devastation. There was a shooting at Sandy Hook Elementary School and 26 people were killed. We all wonder *why?* Hearts wrenched and wounded, is it any wonder why we self-protect and just look out for ourselves and quit believing in good? This is why our hearts grow numb, why we die that way and why we don't bother with the small attempts. Because what's the point, really?

But there's that one word, the Name, the God-man who left Heaven and came down for the express purpose of entering into our pain. He's called the "Man of Sorrows and acquainted with grief."[103]

He didn't have to be. He could have stayed far removed. He didn't have to enter the womb or a woman, grow up to climb the mountain, speak the Good News to a broken world, make Himself bread, and become the Lamb who took stripes for us and now promises to never, *ever* leave us. **He didn't have to do any of that—*but He did.***

He wept. He didn't run from the hopeless, evil, dark pain of our lives stretching out endlessly before us. *Instead, He entered into it so that He could overcome it and give us our heart back.*[104] We really can believe there is good because there is a God. There really is a future and a hope because there is Jesus. Life really is worth living.

*Where is God?* We wonder.

And I have no answers but a word—Jesus. Emmanuel. Bread of Life. The freely given Shepherd and Savior. Close to the broken-hearted. Binder of wounds. Healer. Sustainer, Weeper, and Empathizer. The Comforter. Light in our darkness. The Way, Truth, and Life. Redeemer. Overcomer. Victorious One. The Pearl of Great Price. Lamb of God.

---

[103] Isaiah 53:3
[104] John 16:33

He's everything, and He's right here with us.

And in our moments of exposure, when all the safety nets and securities are removed, in that place where we understand how close we really are to thin air, we can see Him.

# ~Final Word~

It has been a pleasure to walk this journey with you, my friend. I would love to hear from you! You can connect with me on my blog at www.arabahjoy.com. May I pray for you now?

Father, may this reader be strengthened in her faith, may she hold to the promises You have given and stand firm upon Your character; may she be fully convinced of what is unseen, confident of the blessed hope we have in You; may the imperfect and weak words of this book encourage and strengthen and exhort each reader to turn the eyes fully to Jesus, and may each one of us be able to genuinely say, "I trusted in the Lord and was not disappointed." For the glory of Christ and exaltation of Your worthy Name, Amen.

For a list of recommended faith-building resources, please visit www.arabahjoy.com/trust-resources/

You are also invited to listen to the Trust Without Borders podcast, either on iTunes or by visiting www.arabahjoy.com/podcast/

# Other Resources by Arabah Joy

### Complete
(A 21-Day devotional journey on complete in Christ)

### Energy Explosion
A 7-Day Guide to Jump Start Your Energy

### The Family Table
(A free family resource for those who subscribe to my blog. You can get your free copy of this beautiful resource to use around your family table by visiting www.arabahjoy.com/family-table.)

### Abide
Coming Soon!
(A mini Bible study on living from our position in Christ)

To find out more about these resources, visit www.arabahjoy.com or search Amazon.com.

CPSIA information can be obtained
at www.ICGtesting.com
Printed in the USA
LVHW032230181218
600995LV00019B/3216/P

9 781499 638806